Reviewe

"If ever there were a comprehensive book written about dementia, this exceptional paper-back is it. This is truly a well-researched book and Louise Morse is to be congratulated on going way beyond 'the extra mile'. I endorse the note on the back cover, 'Every GP should read this book!' And I would go further: so should we all."

Cambrensis, Amazon.co.uk

"As a carer for a dementia patient I found the Frank and Linda story to be so helpful in articulating and describing the incremental nature of the illness. Its real strength is in showing the Christian response and context in which the disease can be confronted, which is so contrary to the secular response. Read this book and recharge the batteries of hope, but ensure you have a tissue handy as you read some of the moving moments of reality in dealing with dementia."

AJ, Amazon.co.uk

"As we are dealing with two people with dementia this book was extremely helpful. Full of 'helps' and information, this book would be a wonderful resource to those with family or friends who are suffering in this way."

D.M. Lodge, Amazon.co.uk.

"This is a book everyone should read, including doctors, nurses and all healthcare workers."

A. Kid's Review, Amazon.co.uk

DEMENTIA:
Frank and Linda's Story

New Understanding,
New Approaches, New Hope

Louise Morse

MONARCH
BOOKS
Oxford, UK & Grand Rapids, Michigan, USA

First published in the UK in 2010 by Monarch Books
(a publishing imprint of Lion Hudson plc)
Wilkinson House, Jordan Hill Road, Oxford OX2 8DR, England
Tel: +44 (0)1865 302750 Fax: +44 (0)1865 302757
Email: monarch@lionhudson.com
www.lionhudson.com

Reprinted 2010.

ISBN 978 1 85424 930 2

Distributed by:
UK: Marston Book S   gdon, Oxon, OX14 4YN
USA: Kregel Publica   07, Grand Rapids, Michigan 49501

The text paper used in this book has been made from wood
independently certified as having come from sustainable forests.

British Library Cataloguing Data
A catalogue record for this book is available from the British Library.

Printed and bound in the UK by CPI Cox & Wyman, Reading.

Published jointly with Pilgrim Homes, 175 Tower Bridge Road, London SE1 2AL

Contents

Foreword

I am pleased to have read this book, and I recommend it to anyone who wants to learn more about dementia.

Some forty years ago when I was training at The Bethlem Royal Hospital, I was "posted to Siberia" to work as senior registrar in a unit with forty eight elderly patients, for nearly three years. To my surprise it was warm and friendly and I enjoyed working with depressed and demented patients. One day a tired care assistant joined the lunchtime staff meeting, and said "this place is getting like Bedlam". We explained to her that it *was* Bedlam.

Just as the Bethlem had moved on from the Bedlam founded seven centuries earlier (we now had dementia retraining programmes for our patients) so also the care of our elderly patients has changed vastly in the last few decades.

When my mother began to suffer dementia, I learned much more of the problems in caring for her at home. One of my sisters who had cared for our mother herself later died this year, aged ninety, after years of sad suffering with a similar type of dementia. The experiences of what it was like to try and get help from hospitals and care homes for her taught us all much more about dementia.

So, for professional and personal reasons, I was delighted to find in this book many of these problems described in a way which is easy to read. By following one couple (Frank and Linda) the journey of dementia comes alive, and the author illustrates it with many other examples of how to help caregivers and their loved ones who are losing their memories, whose personalities are disintegrating and whose behaviour may be agitated and aggressive at times.

We used to teach medical students that the four letter word in late life problems was *loss*. This book is especially good at explaining the grief of seeing a loved one being "lost" over a period of months or years with dementia. The grief and loss can become all-pervasive. At such times we all need help from relatives, friends and the community – especially, for Christians, the community of believers.

The reader will find all kinds of helpful information laid out in an attractive form in this book. It shows how bureaucracy can hinder and misdirect the obtaining of help. Only those who know enough can fight for justice for those oppressed with dementia.

This book, with its many examples of the good and bad in caring, its fresh and up-to-date views on how caregivers themselves should be helped more, and its skill in showing how modern technology can help (with the "wandering" patient, or in the constant need for observation of patients who get lost in their own homes) – all this provides a rich mix.

It may challenge many of us to increase knowledge and understanding, to motivate us all to offer more T L C (in the full sense of *tender loving care*) and give us the new hope that the book's title suggests we should look for. The book comes out of many years of work for better care of the elderly.

I hope it helps us all to work together to help solve what will be hugely important problems in the next decades, because of the increased numbers of us who grow older.

Though the book is written for Christians, I consider it to

be helpful to anyone who wants to learn more and get better care.

It should be required reading for all those who hold any responsibility for the care of the elderly – including in particular Christian leaders and teachers – and it will be of great encouragement to the caregivers who read it.

Dr Gaius Davies
Consultant Psychiatrist

Introduction
A Sense of Purpose

The Lord will fulfil his purpose for me; your love, O Lord, endures forever...

PSALM 138:8

Is this book for you?

If you are part of the human race and living on planet earth, then the answer is yes. Not just because no man is an island and, as John Donne wrote, when the bell tolls, it tolls "for thee", but because the hard statistics show that in a very short time every family on earth will be affected, one way or another, by dementia. In just over thirty years' time, say the experts, one in three people in the UK will either be a sufferer, a carer, or a relative. Whether your encounter is of the first, the second, or the third kind, this book is designed to give you a better understanding and encouragement. Scientists, public health specialists and governments are coming to grips with dementia, and good things are happening.

In the following chapters you will meet Frank and Linda; real people whose names have been changed. You'll read how they coped with the challenge of dementia: the help they received, or didn't, their good days and their bad days. You'll also meet, in passing, some of the people who have reviewed the chapters. They are specialists in their own fields, all of which touch in some way on the topics covered here, and their insights have been included and attributed in the narrative. The note that follows this chapter describes them briefly: do read it so that you'll know who they are when you see them mentioned.

The 2009 World Alzheimer's Report estimates that 35 million people worldwide are living with dementia. This is predicted to rise to 65.7 million by 2030 and 115.4 million by 2050 – 10 per cent higher than the last Alzheimer's Disease International (ADI) predictions in *The Lancet* in 2005. In Australia it's expected to rise by 400 per cent, said the Alzheimer's Australia education specialist John Price at a conference in July 2009. The global increase is greater than scientists predicted a few years ago because earlier research underestimated dementia's growing impact in developing countries. In poorer countries "dementia is a hidden issue", said Dr Daisy Acosta, who heads the ADI, "and that's complicating efforts to improve earlier diagnosis… You're not supposed to talk about it."

Wrong! In this book we talk about three important aspects of dementia – understanding it, helping and caring. Scientists aren't sure what causes dementia (there are up to 100 causes, although Alzheimer's is implicated in over 58 per cent), and although a number of drugs are undergoing clinical trials, to date there is no cure. "Developing and testing a drug takes 20 years on average from the scientific discovery to the treatment actually being available to people with dementia," says an article on an Alzheimer's website ("A Year in Drugs' Trials", February 2009),[1] but it gives little hard information about any new progress. Dementia is largely a condition of the over-65s, and with populations ageing fast all over the world, meeting their needs clearly gives pharmaceutical companies and researchers a strong sense of purpose.

Knowing our purpose

"I thought you'd be interested in my story," the letter began. It was from a lady who had been to our conference on dementia. She had seen our advertisement and felt led to attend. She wrote:

> My mother had Alzheimer's and I knew it could be hereditary. I bought your book, too.[2] I had been referred to the Memory Clinic and had a scan on my brain. So my husband and I came to the conference never knowing that on our return the scan would reveal that my brain had shrunk. And eventually, out came the "dementia" word! I've struggled very much to cope… some days it's unbearable and I just have to rest. It's not good quality of life with Alzheimer's.

Then she wrote:

> BUT, THE LORD IS GREAT, and through Alzheimer's He has become so much more precious than before! He is giving me such joy and comfort as I read His word – beautiful promises and assurances. I have to speak at a ladies' meeting at the end of the month, and it will be about my journey into Alzheimer's with Jesus!

The Bible describes us as people on pilgrimage, and there are times when our journey takes us through some tough places. But we don't go through them alone. Jesus said that after he had been crucified and gone to heaven, he would send us his Holy Spirit, who would be *in* us, not merely resting on us or alongside us (John 14:17). He promised that the Holy Spirit would never leave us, and our experiences of caring for people with dementia show this to be true. There was the mother who hadn't spoken for nearly two years who, just before she died, said to her daughter, "Remember, God never forgets you. He never forgets you." There is the frail resident who sits, apparently lost in her own world, who responds with bright, knowing eyes as a visitor takes her hand and gently repeats Scripture verses to her. There are the times, during devotions, when faces, normally vacant, light up and frail old voices sing familiar hymns and choruses. God is not some distant aspiration but actually lives in us: he has promised that nothing will separate us from him and his love; nothing, not even dementia (Romans 8:35–39)).

Solomon wrote, "To everything there is a season, a time for every purpose under heaven" (Ecclesiastes 3:1 NKJV). None of us would anticipate a season that might take us on a journey through dementia. It makes no sense to us. Yet neither do children dying in childhood, or young men and women dying on the battlefield. There is so much that we don't understand. We do know, though, that the longer we live, the more we see the principles of Scripture working in our lives, and one day we will see the whole of God's purpose.

In this Introduction we will look at the importance of knowing that, whatever happens to us, our lives have a purpose. Then we will look at the progress that is being made with dementia and the way the most important changes have been brought about by people motivated by love. The Introduction ends with news of an insightful way of caring that helps to take the dread out of dementia. It seems to have sprung up simultaneously in slightly different forms around the world, but it's been systematized in the UK by Penny Garner, a professional carer with some thirty years' experience.

One of the speakers at our 2008 dementia conference was Dr Daphne Wallace, a retired old-age psychiatrist who had been diagnosed with vascular dementia herself a few years earlier. Speaking of adjusting after being given the diagnosis, she said:

> It takes time to adjust, and then to learn to be positive about living with dementia. And if you have an early diagnosis then you have time to come to terms with it. And quite apart from any practical arrangements, you can deal with the experience. We need a sense of purpose; we need to have some sense of the direction we're going in, in our lives.

When we have committed our lives to Christ, we know the direction we're going in. The trouble is that we confuse purpose with achievement. We see this in many older people who say, "I'm no use to anyone any more." It isn't true: the reason our lives have a purpose is because we are here on purpose. One of the greatest evils of evolutionary theory is that it removes from humankind any sense of meaning for their lives, for if we came about by accident, what purpose can we have in being?

Yet we were planned even before the world was made (Ephesians 1:4–5). "In Your book they all were written, the days fashioned for me, when as yet there were none of them", says Psalm 139:16 (NKJV). One of our purposes, according to the writer of the letter to the Ephesians, is that we are to be "to the praise of his glory" (Ephesians 1:12, 14). I particularly

15

like the way the 1647 Westminster Shorter Catechism puts it: "Man's chief end is to glorify God, and to enjoy Him forever." Taken at its face value, if we do nothing but praise God's glory, we are living up to our purpose. And "enjoy Him forever" has a wonderful ring about it. One of the delights of elderly Christians is when they reminisce about their lives, recounting God's goodness and faithfulness, and you only have to see people with dementia calming down as Grace is said before meals, or beaming as they listen to hymns or Scripture, to know that "forever" is not unrealistic. Journeying through dementia means losing much of what we've taken for granted all our lives, except the most important of all – the companionship of the Holy Spirit.

More and more books are being written by people who have dementia themselves. None describe a sense of purpose and eternity better than those written by Christine Bryden,[3] who was a high-flying government executive when she was diagnosed with dementia in 1995. Speaking at a conference in Australia, she said:

> I believe that people with dementia are making an important journey from cognition, through emotion, into spirit. I've begun to realize what really remains through this journey is what is really important. I think that if society could appreciate this, then people with dementia would be treasured and accepted.

Developments in dementia

We've a long way to go before people with dementia feel treasured and accepted, but we've come a long way from the

1980s, when dementia sufferers were treated as though the person had already died and only the shell was left. Care then, such as it was, was degrading and inhumane. Only now is dementia beginning to emerge from the shroud of ignorance and dread. "No cure for Alzheimer's, but we could start by treating sufferers with the sympathy and respect they deserve",[4] was a headline in the *Guardian* newspaper. "Dementia sufferers feel alienated because of a stigma attached to their disease",[5] echoed the *Daily Telegraph* a few days earlier.

"It's something that taps into our big fear of loss of control," said Niall Hunt, the Chief Executive of the King's Fund charity. "The natural reaction to something frightening is to push it to one side."[6] Pushed to one side was how families felt as they struggled to cope. Every week there were stories in the media about caregivers stretched to the limit because they were unable to get help or support. One man, utterly exhausted and run to the emotional wire by his unresponsive Local Authority, took his elderly mother suffering with dementia to the Civic Centre offices and left her there. Newsreader Angela Rippon wrote about the bureaucratic nightmare facing dementia carers. "You become a carer almost by default. It sets you off on a steep learning curve, often alone and without professional help. You are entering unknown territory," she told a dementia conference. Addressing the Royal College of Nursing, veteran television interviewer Sir Michael Parkinson spoke movingly of his mother who had suffered with dementia before she died at the age of ninety-six, and called for better treatment and more dignity.

But things are beginning to change. It's due in part to the sheer weight of numbers in an ageing population where more and more people are reaching the "dementia zone". It is not something that can be ignored, or pushed aside. It will strike one in four people over the age of eighty, and experts have likened it to a tsunami that could cause the public health sector to collapse.

In response, the British government has launched a national dementia strategy to strengthen every aspect of care, from diagnosis to practical support. Its stated aims are tackling ageism and stigmatisation, better dementia training for doctors, early diagnosis, and real support for sufferers and carers. It's not before time, according to a report published by the Nuffield Council on Bioethics nine months after the government's announcement. It warned that dementia patients are still being left with no support after diagnosis, saying it found "ample evidence" that, in many cases, patients are diagnosed and then "simply told to come back in a year's time". "Such a lack of information and support in the immediate aftermath of diagnosis is simply morally wrong," the report emphasized. It also highlighted the unfairness of the current care system, where the needs of people with dementia are classed as "social", and funded accordingly, "despite the fact that the direct cause of their symptoms is progressive damage to the brain." People with cancer are treated far better, it says.[7]

Prodded into responding, the Department of Health issued a statement saying:

We are committed to improving early diagnosis and directing people to the right support, information and advice as soon as possible. We also want to see the stigma attached to dementia tackled at every level, from GPs [family doctors] to friends and family. Our first dementia advisers are now being recruited across the country. They will be a permanent point of contact throughout a person's care and someone they can trust

18

to help them navigate the care and support system, directing them to information they need.[8]

It's progress of a kind: long drawn out and snail-like, but still progress. Previously, there had been no official acknowledgement of the extent of the problem, or of the needs of sufferers and their caregivers. Travelling the road of dementia care is slow, but at least the signposts have been put in place so we know the direction we should be going.

Dismantling the demon

Whether we like it or not, we live in a media-driven world, but it has served us well in this instance. Through the media we've shared the anguish of dozens of celebrities as dementia impacted their lives, and the response has been a global outpouring of sympathy. Celebrities are people we feel we know almost as personal friends, and we care about what happens to them. In America, the first lady of California, Maria Shriver, is making a four-part documentary, *The Alzheimer's Project*, after her father developed dementia. Her aim, she said, is to lift some of the fear, shame, guilt and confusion that surround the disease. In the UK journalists, TV presenters and newsreaders have told their stories, and John Suchet, British TV presenter and author, spoke of his grief as his wife Bonnie struggled with the illness. "I've lost my Bonnie," he told the world on BBC news: she has "gone from him", although she's still alive.

Dementia has been "demonized" more than any other illness, and perhaps the celebrity who did most to cut it down to size was someone who's been diagnosed with it himself, the bestselling author, Terry Pratchett. Sir Terence Pratchett,

OBE, to give him his full name, has sold more than 55 million books worldwide, and is the second most-read writer in the UK and the seventh most-read non-US author in the USA. He has millions of fans of all ages, and they are inordinately fond of him.

He was diagnosed with a rare form of Alzheimer's that affects the part of the brain that deals with vision: posterior cortical atrophy. Although people didn't talk about dementia because they found it so frightening, he insisted:

> The first step is to talk openly about dementia because it's a fact, well enshrined in folklore, that if we are to kill the demon then first we have to say its name. Once we have recognised the demon, without secrecy or shame, we can find its weaknesses. It's a physical disease, not some mystic curse; therefore it will fall to a physical cure.

It was an irony that the man whose books could not be categorized at first because they were outside the accepted genres should now be thrusting into the spotlight a condition that has not fitted a neat slot in either the public understanding or public health services. His work has been compared with Jonathan Swift's. Both portray the idiosyncrasies of the human race by observing them with humour and compassion in a parallel universe; in Pratchett's case, mainly (but not exclusively) from the cities of the Discworld.

Some years ago I interviewed a group of scientists in what is probably the biggest global corporation in the world. I was working on an article about the applications of a particular type of "neural networking" software and the scientists had agreed to talk about its place in their work. We found, almost to a man, that we were all Pratchett readers and, as well as an extraordinarily good-humoured meeting, we shared a language with a hinterland that provided shortcuts to describing what they were doing. It was probably fans like these that Pratchett had in mind when he said that only his family and the fact that he had fans in the medical profession who gave him useful advice got him through "that moment" when he was given the diagnosis. His huge fan base has given him the kind of access to people in research and clinical trials that would be closed to the rest of us. Although other famous people have spoken out, it's usually because they have partners or parents who have been affected.

When it comes to Terry Pratchett, though, the thinking seems to be that if dementia can strike someone like him and he will stand up and speak about it, then it isn't something disgraceful; and if he is prepared to go public and argue for better research, and implicitly, better understanding, then it's OK for others to speak openly about it, too. It is probably little consolation to him but, because he's so well liked and appreciated, by changing the public perception of dementia and prompting a greater willingness to tackle it, he has done more to slay the demon than most.

Lighting a better way

Until there is a cure, the emphasis will be on care. More than most conditions, in dementia the care is the treatment, for the brain, far from being a rigid, mechanical structure, responds physically to the treatment the person receives. It can be damaged, or encouraged to grow new pathways. This was noted by Professor Tom Kitwood, a psychiatrist and clinical psychologist at Bradford University, as far back as 1997 (in his book *Dementia Reconsidered*), when he wrote that a poor, social environment "may actually be damaging to nerve tissue. Dementia may be induced, in part, by the stresses of life... Maintaining personhood is both a psychological and a neurological task."[9]

Tom Kitwood introduced the concept of "person-centred care", moving the focus from the medical mindset, occupied with deficits and pathology, to the individual. His approach is being adopted gradually throughout the public sector, though how much is still lip service is hard to tell. A busy ward with constantly changing nurses with very little time to study, let alone apply, a detailed care plan can hardly be ideal, and it is probably true to say that with the NHS now focusing more on cure than care, older people with dementia are best cared for in residential care homes with a family ethos and well-trained staff. Now, a new approach has been defined that takes Tom Kitwood's concepts to a new level.

It was developed by Penny Garner, the professional carer mentioned earlier, who also cared for her mother when she developed dementia. It's explained in the book *Contented Dementia*, written by clinical child psychologist Oliver James, who happens to be her son-in-law. He says he is so impressed by Penny's method, SPECAL, that if he were to develop dementia, he would be perfectly fine as long as his mother-in-law looked after him.[10]

SPECAL stands for Specialised Early Care for Alzheimer's, but is equally helpful for all forms of dementia. It's a deeply empathetic but very practical approach based on knowing as much about the individual as possible. At the core of SPECAL is the ability to identify what is happening in the individual's inner landscape, recognizing that where they are now living in their minds is as real as where we are – but theirs is in the past and ours is in the present. By knowing their life themes and core beliefs it's possible to make a link with the past to the present.

An example is the story of Jack. He was chatting to another person at the Day Unit when, for no apparent reason, he dived under the table and cowered there, shivering with fright. SPECAL sense is opposite to common sense. The common-sense response was to bend down, ask Jack if he was all right and suggest he come out, which would have only made him more agitated.[11] Using her SPECAL sense, Penny Garner joined him, casually, under the table and said nothing for a moment, wondering what was going on in his mind. She searched her memory for what she knew of Jack and, remembering his tough wartime experiences, realized that he was taking shelter under the table, waiting for danger to pass. It made perfect sense in his world. (The danger signal turned out to be clanging saucepans from the nearby kitchen.) Penny Garner was careful to validate Jack's concern and not challenge the sense that he had made of the situation, and by understanding what was going on in his mind she was able to see a way out and make a link back to the present. After waiting a while and chattering empathetically, she said that it was all clear now and they had better go and get their mugs of tea very quickly before someone else drank them.

Reports are that the SPECAL method works well. The Royal College of Nursing say that their dementia patients take fewer drugs and experience less distress. It promotes well-being and makes life bearable and easier for carers and clients. It even helps to maintain the client's unique personality, which in itself is a great blessing for their loved ones. People with dementia do not get better, but in Penny Garner's experience

23

they can live contentedly. One of Pilgrim Homes' trustees, Roger Hitchings, used to be Director of Age Concern in Birmingham, and ran the largest Day Care Unit in the UK for Alzheimer's sufferers. He also speaks from personal experience, as his mother died of dementia. He studied at the London Bible College and is now a pastor, and brings spiritual insight as well as practical experience when he counsels families, or give talks at conferences. He recommends Oliver James' book and the SPECAL approach. We refer to SPECAL in various places, and recommend that you buy a copy of the book.[12]

No one in history has shown more compassion and care for people than Jesus Christ. When he wept at the tomb of his friend Lazarus, I believe he was grieved to his core at the sorrow that sickness brings in the world. I wonder if he felt sad at the very thought of bringing Lazarus back into it. This same Jesus, who empathized so deeply then, is still the same today.

In the coming chapters we will show how today's newly defined way of caring corresponds well with Christian care. For Christians share the same core beliefs, have similar life narratives and in many cases have sung, literally, from the same song-sheet. Scripture verses and Christian songs are strong links in time and reality, and God is glorified as beliefs are reaffirmed. We see how it works as we follow Frank and Linda through their journey with dementia.

If the book raises questions, you can leave them on the Message Board at our website, www.pilgrimhomes.org.uk, and if we don't have a ready answer, we'll find someone who does. You can share your own stories, too.

Prayer

by the Rt Revd Bishop James Jones of Liverpool

Lord
In weakness or in strength
We bear your image.
We pray for those we love
Who now live in a land of shadows
Where the light of memory is dimmed
Where the familiar lies unknown
Where the beloved become as strangers.
Hold them in your everlasting arms and
Grant to those who care
A strength to serve
A patience to persevere
A love to last
And a peace that passes human understanding.
Hold us in your everlasting arms
Today and for all eternity
Through Jesus Christ our Lord
Amen.

Who We Are

The purpose of this little note is to introduce you to the people whose names you'll find here and there throughout the book. We're all pilgrims; that is, we are in the company of those mentioned in Hebrews 12:1 who are on a journey through life on our way to heaven.

You may remember myself and *Roger Hitchings* from our book *Could it Be Dementia? Losing Your Mind Doesn't Mean Losing Your Soul*. I'm a former journalist with a diploma in marketing and a Christian counsellor and Cognitive Behavioural Therapist, as well as Media and Communications Manager for Pilgrim Homes. Roger is a trustee of Pilgrim Homes and pastor of East Leake Evangelical Church in the East Midlands. Before training in Theology at the London School of Theology he was Director of Age Concern in Birmingham where, amongst many other activities, he managed the largest Day Care Unit for Alzheimer sufferers in the country. He was also Director of the Bristol Royal Society for the Blind, working extensively in the fields of ageing and disability.

Janet Jacob is a Registered Mental Nurse, whose career has been spent in Psychogeriatric Nursing. She is a former Homes' Manager for Pilgrim Homes, and is now the Deputation Co-ordinator for the society. She takes seminars and gives talks at conferences and in churches.

Penny Garner is the founder and Clinical Lead of SPECAL.

She reviewed and contributed to Chapter 8, 'Passport to Care', and I'm very grateful to her. SPECAL is an independent charity to promote lifelong well-being for people with dementia, based in Burford, Oxfordshire. The website is www.specal.co.uk, and fuller contact details are given at the back of the book.

Deborah Steiner is a London-based freelancer, and works for Christian charities in communications areas ranging from media writing to blog management. She also takes an active role in anti-slavery campaigning.

Gwen Stewart is a former teacher, missionary and magazine editor. She has been closely associated with Pilgrim Homes for a long time, and used to edit our *Quarterly Record*. She's been retired for many years but is still involved in some writing and enjoys being a grandma. She is a good grammarian and one of those who, like me, tips a hat to Strunk and White, the doyens of style.

Fran Waddams is a Theology graduate who began her teaching career thirty years ago and currently teaches Religious Studies in Lincoln. She manages a large "A" Level Religious Studies website and is an Assistant Examiner for Religious Studies at "A" Level.

Kim Todd trained as a doctor and worked for some years as a general practitioner and now does voluntary work for a charity called Lovewise, which involves going into schools to talk about marriage, sex and relationships, a cause which she is passionate about.

Judy McLaren is a busy general practitioner and a trustee of Pilgrim Homes.

Judith Sly trained as an English teacher, then later moved into Social Services, where she often had contact with clients suffering from dementia. She reviews this book from the heart, as her mother lived out her last few years in a residential nursing home where there was no Christian fellowship. Judith and her husband Peter run a Christian writers' group.

Carol Bradley Bursack is an American columnist and speaker, and author of *Minding Our Elders: Caregivers Share Their Personal Stories*. Carol has contributed to the chapter, "Letter from America". Her newspaper column runs weekly in print and online, she speaks at workshops and conferences and has been interviewed by national radio, newspapers and magazines. Carol writes for several elder care websites, moderates caregiving forums and is the editor-in-chief of ElderCarelink.com. Her sites are www.mindingourelders.com and www.mindingoureldersblogs.com.

Psalm 84:5 says, "Blessed are those whose strength is in you, who have set their hearts on pilgrimage," and we all say "Amen" to that.

Chapter 1

A Day at a Time

I can do all things through Christ who strengthens me...

Being able to cope with all that life brings our way through God's grace had been the theme of the pastor's sermon that morning, and it was Linda's silent prayer as she backed nervously into her neighbour's driveway, doing her best to ignore Frank's directions from the passenger seat. She disliked driving at the best of times, but reversing was the thing she hated most. Normally she avoided it, but because their house was on an awkward bend in the road, Frank insisted they should drive out bonnet first, which meant backing in beforehand. Worst of all was that Frank (not for the first time) mistook their neighbour's driveway for their own, and insisted on directing her into it. It was no use protesting because he would explode with anger – the anger that had seemed to lodge in him ever since he'd had to give up his driving licence because of his dementia. Frank had always been their driver, and when Linda had had to take over he would either sit morosely or take to barking directions like an ill-tempered Sat Nav. It was like trying to pacify a bear while running off with its cub. Although she was getting better at distracting him and changing his mood, when she was on edge as she was now, it took all her energy simply to get the job done.

She thanked God she hadn't damaged their neighbour's roses. Frank didn't notice that their neighbour's driveway was lined with rose bushes, while theirs was clear. It was just another of the anomalies caused by the dementia. She thanked God, too, for sympathetic neighbours who understood what was happening. They had lived next door to each other for years, and had known Frank BD – Before Dementia. They'd known him as he had been for most of his life: affable and capable, and that helped a lot.

Nowadays Linda found herself thanking God more often than she had ever done – which was amazing, she thought, now that she had more to cope with than at any other time in her life. She was so grateful that she knew, without a shadow of doubt, that God was real and that he cared for her. She hadn't been raised in a Christian household, and like millions of others, she had found God by searching. In her early twenties she'd decided that there had to be more to life than this, and had set out to find the meaning of life. A tall order, she'd often thought on reflection, but when you're young you feel anything is possible. She researched secretly, borrowing books from the library about religions old and new, other cultures, and philosophy. But none held the answer. Then she came across a New Testament, and began to read it as she waited for dinner to finish cooking. Four hours later she was still reading. Some of the pages were spattered with Bolognese sauce because she'd read right through dinner, hardly taking her eyes off, winding the spaghetti on to her fork without looking. "It was an encounter with the Holy Spirit," she said afterwards. "It all made so much sense. Jesus said he was the way, the truth and the life, so I'd found the meaning I was looking for." She wouldn't claim to understand the whole of life and some things that happened were beyond her understanding, but then, human understanding was limited even in the cleverest of people. The basis of both her life and Frank's, who'd come to faith before they met, was their relationship with Jesus Christ.

Now, almost fifty years later, she hurried to reach her front door before her husband became anxious because he couldn't find the key he didn't have any more. Another "Thank you, Lord" when she got there first. Once inside, she suggested having a cup of tea, adding, "Let's see if there's anything interesting on television for you." She switched on the set while he made himself comfortable in his favourite chair and, wanting him to be completely absorbed, she popped one of his favourite old films into the DVD player. As the music swelled with the *Dam Busters* theme she said, "I'll go and make that tea now." Frank nodded as she left the room, and she went quickly through the front door, locking it again behind her. "Lord, keep him contented," she breathed. It meant the dreaded reversing again, this time into their own drive. It would only take a few minutes and Frank usually didn't notice the time it took to make the tea, but there was always the chance that he might forget what she'd said and start looking for her, going from room to room. Today, though, he stayed engrossed in the *Dam Busters*, looking up briefly when she placed his teacup on the side table.

Life before and after dementia

For Linda, the contrast between life before dementia, or BD, and afterwards, AD, was almost beyond description. BD, everything had been so simple, so normal and ordinary. AD, life was incredibly complicated and highly strung, like walking a tightrope and juggling a dinner service at the same time. Whereas BD, most of the day would go by on autopilot as it did for most people, AD life called for major strategies, sometimes two or three in the space of five minutes. Some were to head off an anxious situation, as she had with the front door keys; some were to divert or distract him; some were about choosing the best option at the moment; or sometimes it was simply trying to match what was going on in his mind with different answers or suggestions. She was glad that she was good at multi-tasking, but she often felt like the Italian traffic conductor in the television commercial, using all her energy to direct traffic but without the luxury of being able to step down from the podium to take whatever it was the person was taking to relieve tension.

Even the simplest thing could be unbelievably complicated, such as helping Frank put his socks on in the morning. It could take several attempts because he would say they weren't his socks, or they weren't a matching pair, or they didn't feel right. On other days he made no fuss and they would go straight on. Frank was often at his best in the morning, though they were not the best times for Linda because her arthritis was worst then. She wondered how much longer she could keep going like this. Six months ago she'd turned seventy, and Frank was seventy-two. He was sixty-six when he'd been diagnosed with dementia, caused by a combination of vascular dementia and Alzheimer's disease. But Linda thought the signs that something was going wrong had been there several years before, when Frank began to have trouble finding the right word, or would forget things and repeat himself. It was as if his mental gears were not meshing, and he took longer to work things out. He was also struggling with depression. His driving had begun to change then, too – imperceptible little changes at first. He seemed to hug the centre line in the road and, although he'd always been a good navigator, he began to lose the way even on familiar routes. It would make Linda nervous, though she would try to hide it because it would make him anxious – something he'd never been behind the wheel. They'd put it all down, then, to the fact that he was planning for retirement two years earlier than he'd expected because of redundancies within the company, and coping with a major life change.

"We're not as young as we used to be," they would tell each other, but there were so many small but significant changes in him that she knew, in her heart, that something was not right. "It must be this depression," she would reason with herself.

Our earthly tent

The word "dementia" derives from a Latin word which means, literally, apart from, or away from the mind. It's not a mental illness; it's a progressive degeneration of the brain that is incurable and irreversible. Our brains are probably the most important part of our bodies, because they are our control centre, like the bridge of a ship. We know that the way we communicate and project ourselves to others is enabled by different parts of the brain, and when it is damaged that ability to project is impaired.

Does that mean that the individual, the person known to God, has changed? Most emphatically it does not. From the biblical point of view we understand that if our personalities, the essence of who we are, were the result of the brain we genetically inherit then, when the brain died, so would we. It would be "lights out" for us: the end. But if, as Jesus Christ promised, there is life after physical death with him and, by the sound of it, a better life than most people currently enjoy, then clearly our brains, like the rest of our bodies, are the controls we use to interact with the physical world. When they are damaged our ability to project who we are and what we want to communicate is damaged.

It is important to remember this, because the worst thing for families and carers, and possibly the cruellest aspect of dementia, is watching what seems to be the slow disintegration of a loved one's personality. Their behaviour changes and they say and do things they have never done before. But put yourself in their shoes for a moment. Try this – imagine you are an advanced-skills driving instructor, and have great pleasure in owning and driving a top-of-the-range car, say a Jaguar. You prefer a manual gearbox because an automatic gearbox doesn't have the feel or precision that you do. People look to you as a source of excellence and come to you for advice, and probably your insurance premiums are lower than average because of your skills and reputation. Family holidays have always been a special delight, as you drive with ease across continents, eschewing Sat Navs because map reading is second nature to you. Then you develop dementia. The road maps look like a children's maze and you start getting lost, even in familiar places; the gearstick might as well be a pudding spoon; and instead of an elegant manoeuvre when you park, you start curbing your tyres and clipping other cars. You start avoiding places where you need to park; instead of confidence you ooze anxiety and frustration. Your behaviour has changed – but have you? No, the essence of who you are, the person known to God, has not changed – you are the same "you". But the controls that you used to communicate with your world are becoming unreliable and, conversely, the same controls that fed you back information that made sense of your world are no longer working well, either.

Linda's husband Frank had always been an easygoing, good-natured man, but as the dementia developed there were times when he would become angry and frustrated. At first Linda put it down to the dementia, but she quickly realized that the frustration came from things that Frank found himself unable to do. And she saw that the anger surfaced when he felt diminished or disempowered. The most typical trigger would be when she walked around the car to the driver's side. Sometimes he would object, and stand between her and the car door, or try to take the keys from her hand. At first she was startled, and deflected him by making an excuse about going back into the house to look for something she'd forgotten. But the next time she was prepared, and when it happens now she says, "Oh, come on, Frank! You know how I need you to sit beside me and build up my confidence when I'm driving!" There is always a reason for the behaviour. In Frank's case, not only had he been a good driver, but for most of his life he had been the manager of a transport fleet. Knowing Frank, Linda is able to direct him with something that is positive, not negative.

Clinical psychologist Graham Stokes observes that:

> too often the tragic fate of people with dementia is that once they have been diagnosed with dementia everything that happens after the diagnosis is attributed to the diagnosis. The pursuit of "why" is rendered redundant; for the answer is… "it is because they have dementia." This is rarely so.[13]

Exceptions may be where there has been substantial damage in the part of the brain that deals with judgment and controls inhibitions – the frontal lobes of the brain – and even then this is not so much due to personality change as to poor impulse control. As a consequence, emotions are not inhibited and expression is altered. Sometimes we find that older, godly people will use language that has always been anathema to them. It is because our brains record everything that happens in our lives – all the events, people, thoughts and feelings – and the things we do not approve of we will suppress during our lifetimes. Many church workers reach out into groups of people where foul language and blasphemy are commonplace, and they would be remembered with distaste, and not used. But when this part of the brain is damaged, the sufferer loses the ability to exercise judgment and control.

The effect of good or bad care

Good care helps to preserve sufferers' sense of identity and personality, and poor care does the opposite. A lack of compassion and understanding produces emotional isolation. An example is Margaret, who is now living in one of our care homes. She had been living in a nursing home and her family had become concerned because she was becoming more and more withdrawn. She had chosen not to talk, and would sit silent and isolated. The family asked our home manager, Anne, if Margaret could come to live in her care home, as she was a Christian and they thought it might help her. Anne visited her in the nursing home and was dismayed to find her "wedged into a chair, with a curling bacon sandwich on a tray in front of her". For frailer, older people being wedged into a chair is a physical restraint because they don't have the strength to wriggle up and out. Anne suggested to Margaret's family that she should try our home for a day, and she was clearly so happy there that she transferred from the nursing home. Within a day in the loving environment where all her Christian life themes are enacted, where she felt understood and valued, she began to talk again. Now she engages with other "pilgrims" and takes part in the home's activities. The activities in our homes are so many and varied that just thinking about them is exhausting, but they're all designed to keep residents interested and involved, with something for everyone. "It's not good for people with dementia to become withdrawn," Anne states. Withdrawing is something that most people within this manager's orbit would find hard to maintain. Warm and outgoing and passionate about her "pilgrims", she seems to me to be a walking therapy centre in herself.

At this point in their lives, Frank and Linda have not yet considered finding a suitable care home, though they know they may need to think about it later. After they'd been given the diagnosis they discussed the implications and the options open to them, made some decisions and then, Linda said, "We decided to make the most of the time we had left, leaving the worries of tomorrow to tomorrow." They would take life a day at a time.

The couple have a lifelong habit of a short prayer time before going to bed, and then Frank retires first, leaving Linda to tidy up, checking that electrical switches are off and everything is as it should be. She calls it her "bedtime potter". This evening she wondered again how people manage to get through life without knowing God. Even BD, she thought that life was far from plain sailing. How did they manage without that sense of his presence – of knowing that "underneath are the everlasting arms"?[14] But then she thought of the Yorkshire saying that "There's nowt so rum as folk", meaning there's no accounting for people's foibles. As she reviewed the day, which included reversing down next door's drive, she thought again that yes, God did keep his promises – he does give grace, even in the trauma of coping with dementia. She could commit tomorrow to him, too, although she had to pull her mind back from "Italian traffic conductor" mode even as she thought about it. The house needed to be vacuumed and cleaned and Frank would insist on helping, but Linda had a suggestion from her pastor and an idea that she thought might help. And what did Scripture say about not worrying about tomorrow because the worries of the day are enough? "Too true," she said to herself.

POINTS TO PONDER

- Don't argue, or try to reason when someone's perception of reality is not the same as yours. They are not being awkward. Their cognitive ability is diminished, and their reality is different to yours. We will see more of this in later chapters, together with tactics for coping. But if you have specific questions, now or at any stage through this book, leave questions on the Message Board on our website.
- Where appropriate, let others know what is happening, so they can understand and help if possible. In Linda's case, her neighbours understood why her car was in their drive. Let your church and pastor know.
- *Be thankful.* A thankful heart is a receptive heart. You can't be thankful for dementia, but you can be thankful for a faithful God who makes "all things work together" for our good (Romans 8:28). The most extreme example is the Cross.

- Linda didn't ask Frank whether he would like a cup of tea – she made the suggestion. Because people with dementia find it uncomfortable to come up with answers, even to simple questions, it's less frightening for them if you don't ask questions. But you have to use your own judgment, because asking questions respects the person's autonomy. On a good day, when Frank seems brighter, Linda will ask him to choose something – say, tea or coffee: she knows whether it's a good day or a bad day. SPECAL recommends not asking questions at all, but others feel you can't be categorical about this. It depends on the person and the situation. Janet stood for minutes in a store with her mother, waiting for her to choose some sandwich fillings. Her mother grew more unsettled and distressed and Janet realized she couldn't reason well at that moment, so suggested some fillings for her: "You know, Mum, the ham and turkey slices, and the cheese you always like." Her mother's face cleared and she was all right again.

- Linda tries to direct Frank away from challenging situations, as she did with the door key. It helps to think of things in advance. It gets easier with practice.

- Don't put odd behaviour down to the dementia. More and more experts are saying that often the person is doing something that is quite reasonable within their own world (unless, of course, there is damage to the frontal lobes of the brain). A man who kept trying to break the glass and handles on the patio doors in his new care home was desperately trying to get out to the garden. A shy, private man, he loved gardening and hated being indoors, especially with people who were strangers to him. We recommend you buy Dr Stokes' book, *And Still the Music*

Plays. Drawing on his experiences, Dr Stokes shows how the behaviour makes sense when you know what the person is trying to achieve. It's easier when you know the individual well: Linda understands why Frank becomes angry when he can't drive any more.

- Left to themselves, people with dementia will instinctively withdraw, feeling "less than" they were – diminished and worthless. As Linda thinks about involving Frank with the housework, she is giving him positive signals that he is valued by her.

- *Pray!* God knows every thought of your heart, every word on your tongue before you say it, so you can be honest with him. Give him *everything.*

Chapter 2

Truth and Grace

Now all things are of God, who has reconciled us to Himself through Jesus Christ, and has given us the ministry of reconciliation, that is, that God was in Christ reconciling the world to Himself.

2 CORINTHIANS 5:18–19 (NKJV)

One of the most amazing statements the Bible makes is that God himself came into our world to make himself known to us. He is the Creator and, had he wanted to, he could have devised any number of ways of communicating with us, but he chose to come to earth in a human body and as a servant. He spoke in the everyday language of the people he had created. It's good to remember this as we look at ways of understanding and helping people with dementia. If God could take the trouble to leave the wonderful world that he enjoys, with all its glory, to enter the fallen world in which we live, out of love for us, then we can make the effort of entering the fractured world of those with dementia to help them, too. As ever, in his mercy, God shows the way.

Before they moved into their present house Frank and Linda had had a large house which they ran as a guest house. Running it had been a full-time job for Linda, with Frank helping out part time, his main job being with his transport company. Never a man to sit twiddling his thumbs, he was as comfortable with the vacuum cleaner at home as he was with the rear axle of a twelve-wheeler truck at work. When thoughts of retirement crept over the horizon, they decided to sell the guest house and buy something smaller. With just three bedrooms, the new house was much smaller and easier to manage, but they continued their friendly old habit of looking after it together. Now though, Linda wishes Frank would stick to the garden and forget the housework, because when he is helping he does more than whisk around the vacuum cleaner. He collects things and puts them in odd places, sometimes gathering up several items and dropping them in the kitchen bin. Keys disappear, along with small bedside clocks, and Linda finds her spectacles at the bottom of the bread bin. It's no use asking Frank where he's put things because he's forgotten he's moved them, and asking him why he's moving them in the first place unsettles him because he can't find the answer, and his eyes will take on the frightened look Linda so hates to see.

Sometimes she can divert him; if she sees him heading towards the kitchen with a vase of flowers destined for the bin, she will hold out her hands and say, "Well done! Aren't you clever to spot that they need fresh water! Give me the vase and I'll just top it up now." She'll also make sure the kitchen bin is empty and has a clean liner so she can reclaim the items and put them quietly back in their proper places later.

But the moves that give her the most trouble are when Frank rearranges the furniture. He always does it when he is in the room by himself. The first time it had happened when Linda was busy in the kitchen. Coming into the room, she stopped in astonishment, saying that everything had been moved and looked at him questioningly, but he didn't remember doing it and was so confused and anxious that she didn't ask him again.

She assumed it was just one of those odd things that wouldn't happen again, but it did, at least twice a week. Sometimes she could persuade him to move some of the heavier pieces back by suggesting she'd like to try them in a different part of the room, and he'd happily comply. Other times he would be resistant or not interested, so she would wait until he went into the garden or for a walk with a friend, and she'd move it back herself. He didn't seem to notice. Occasionally she'd leave it where he'd moved it, as far as possible, but after a while he'd move it again. She joked to her friends that theirs must be the only furniture in Yorkshire that needed a 10,000-mile service, but her arthritis was getting more painful by the week and as time went on, she looked forward less and less to her moving chore.

It isn't just the furniture that takes Frank's attention. In the supermarket, when they reach the checkout he will place their groceries neatly on the belt, and then turn to the next checkout and begin to arrange the groceries there, too. He will stop when Linda says gently that they aren't theirs, smiling apologetically at the surprised shopper at the same time.

There seems to be no reason why Frank rearranges the furniture or the groceries on the checkout belt. But even though he looked confused and wasn't able to give an answer when Linda asked once why he was doing it, it isn't something he does in a random or absent-minded way. "It seems to mean something to him," she told their son Matthew.

Meaning in behaviour

Moving things was also a daily routine of one of Dr Stoke's patients with Alzheimer's, only in this case it was rocks and stones out of his garden.[15] Mr D. would spend hours each day filling a wheelbarrow and trundling them into the house, dumping them on the carpet. Disregarding flowerbeds and trampling over anything in his way, he gradually decimated his garden and then began on their neighbours'. It made no sense at all to his wife, but any efforts to persuade him to stop would horrify and torment him.

Examining his life history with his wife revealed an incident where Mr D. had once been terrified by burglars who had hurled a large piece of masonry they'd found in a nearby building skip through a window, to break into his business premises. He had been inside at the time and had hidden in a back office. A shy and timid man, he had always been security conscious, but this incident heightened his need to keep everything safe and burglar-proof.

With dementia, memory and understanding fail but feelings remain, often intensified. Years later, now suffering with Alzheimer's, Mr D. was doing his best to keep his wife and his home safe by removing every rock and stone from the immediate vicinity. "Within the limits laid down by his intellectual disability, Mr D. was behaving in a manner that was right and appropriate," Dr Stokes observed.[16] Once they understood this, his family made sure that there were always rocks in their own garden that he could find by replenishing them from the place they had persuaded him to use in a corner of the garage. His family were touched that, in the depths of dementia, he was attempting to keep them safe.

Linda talked about Frank's moving habit with their son Matthew. Like his father, Matthew works in transport, and he wondered if Frank could be repeating something that he used to do dozens of times a day – helping to get consignments lined up ready for despatching. There was always pressure to meet deadlines because an hour late from the despatching bay could translate into a missed time-slot at the customer's end and there could be penalties. Frank would be feeling anxious until everything was ready to roll, but once he'd checked that all was well and in place, he could relax. Now, feeling anxious and not knowing why, he could be looking for relief by repeating what had worked for him almost daily for years and years – moving things into line, ready to be picked up and loaded. In dementia, when a person's motivations are recognized as enduring habits that have been compromised by brain disease, it is referred to as "comfortable behaviour".[17] Perhaps "comforting" would be a better word.

Sitting with others in a doctor's waiting room, Penny Garner's mother thought they were in an airport lounge waiting to be called for their flight. Travel had played a big part in her life and she had many memories of long waits at airports, so this was how she made sense of being in a crowded waiting room. She had no recent memory of arranging to see the doctor, or of being driven to his office. But she had many past memories of sitting in similar crowds, waiting for flights to be called.

A wrong interpretation of someone's behaviour can have disastrous results. Imagine what went through the cook's mind as she entered the nursing home's kitchen and saw one of the residents standing there holding a knife. She pushed the emergency button and he was whisked off to a secure unit where he was heavily sedated. Within months he was dead. Yet if she had only known that he was not deluded and not dangerous, his life could have turned out differently, for Paddy had been a master baker, and as far as he was concerned, he was just getting down to work.

There are probably tens of thousands, if not millions of stories of people with dementia who enact themes from their past lives, like Frank and Paddy. The key is understanding why it makes sense to them. It's more than simply having a lot of information about their past lives; it's being able to walk through their inner landscape, empathising and validating. Christian counsellors depart from Carl Rogers' theory at more than one point, but he was right when he observed that, "The best vantage point for understanding behaviour is from the internal frame of reference of the individual himself."[18]

In putting things in order, Frank is not just mindlessly repeating old tasks, but is looking for the satisfaction of a job well done: Paddy wants to go to work for that feeling of belonging and usefulness, and Mr D. wants to feel secure. Jack, mentioned in the first chapter, wanted to be out of harm's way. Penny Garner's mother Dorothy wanted to feel confident that everything was in order as they waited for the flight.

It's not at all uncommon for people with dementia to want to go back to a job they've retired from many years ago. The doors in our care homes have coded keypads, but they're sometimes not enough to deter a determined resident. One of our homes is in a beautiful rural location and is a destination in itself. One of the residents would sit by the front door, eagle-eyed, waiting for someone to go out. Usually staff spotted her and would divert her attention to something else, but one day she slipped out alongside a new postman. (The old postman would have noticed.) Fortunately she was spotted a mile or so down the country road by one of the carers who was driving in for duty. The carer stopped and said, quite naturally, "Hello, Olive! Going off to work, are you? Would you like a lift? It looks like it might rain in a minute." Although the car was facing back the way she'd come, Olive got happily in and went back home. Often people will set out with a purpose but quickly forget what it was. They still feel the need to be going somewhere, however, so they keep on going. Very rarely does someone with dementia slip away from a care home, but everyone's heart beats faster until they come back!

A better understanding

One of the ways our brains process new information is by relating it to things we already know. But people with dementia are not able to store new information and so short-term memory is defective. The SPECAL approach compares our memory recall system with a photo-album, with the oldest photographs at the bottom. When we "lay down" memories, both facts and feelings are recorded. Often the stronger the feeling, the more we remember; we can usually remember where we were when we heard that Princess Diana had died, for example.

Not being able to store new information means individuals can have no idea where they are or who they are talking to, so to make sense of the present they will search their stored memories for comparable circumstances. Finding something similar, they will be convinced that is where they are now. Their situation will be as real to them as yours is now. And it is a real situation – it isn't something that they are making up. It's just that it is part of their history and it may be something you have no idea about. But it is real. And it is terrifying for them if they are told it is not.

Imagine what it would be like if someone kept telling you that your version of reality was wrong, that you are actually somewhere else or doing something entirely different! Feeling like an actor in a play where all the other actors seem to be performing a different one, you might become terrified and panic stricken or aggressive.

Sometimes people with dementia are misinterpreted as being psychotic or schizophrenic, and anti-psychotic drugs are given, but the drugs don't work because they are wrongly targeted. "Anti-psychotic medication for people with dementias such as Alzheimer's is not only inappropriate, it can be fatal," says psychologist Oliver James, "the psychological damage of these drugs is also huge: they dope, befuddle and reduce communication."[19] Part of the government's dementia strategy is to reduce drastically the amount of anti-psychotic drugs given to patients with dementia, but ten months after the announcement, a survey by the Alzheimer's Society found that they were still being prescribed liberally on hospital wards. The number of patients prescribed the drugs in hospital was likely to be in the order of tens of thousands, according to Neil Hunt, Chief Executive of the Alzheimer's Society.

People with dementia are not psychotic or deluded; they do not claim to be someone other than the person on their birth certificate. The world they are in is a very real world; even though it is in the past, they did not make it up. It's somewhere that is safe and familiar, and if caregivers can learn to enter that world, they can link it with the present, as our carer did when she found Olive going to work, and as Penny Garner did when Jack dived under the table (see the Introduction).

"It's not just about getting them to live in a la-la land in the past, it's about using their past memories to help them to live in the present," said psychologist Oliver James during a BBC interview. "It's enormously practical; you can then convert that into helping them to eat… to do all the practical things in the present today."[20]

Linking with the past works in more ways than one. When one of our residents said she wanted to leave, the manager sat alongside her and put her feet up, encouraging the resident to do the same, and said, "I understand how you feel, Doris. Let's look at this. Let's take a moment and look at how things have worked out in the past." Fortunately, she knew enough about the resident to be able to tap into significant events and, matching them with the present, was able to help Doris feel comfortable about staying. It wasn't the same as entering the person's landscape, and it wasn't a cognitive, reasoning process, but a transfer of positive feelings from similar situations to the present.

Jesus frequently made links between the world of heaven and that of earth. He said the kingdom of heaven belonged to children (Matthew 19:14), and he was very clear when he told the story of the beggar, Lazarus, in heaven, and the rich man, who wasn't. One of the names of Jesus is "the Truth", yet he taught gently in parables, getting alongside people and meeting them where they were. When he talked to the Samaritan woman at the well, he didn't ask probing questions. The compassion and empathy of Jesus is irresistible.

Talking about her fifteen-year experience of caring for her mother, who had Frontal Lobe Dementia, author Charlotte Parker said, "The most essential component is having the willingness to release the attachment we all hold to our individual perceptions of reality and choose to quite literally step into the demented person's reality."

Most of us find it easy to enter a child's world: it's familiar to us because we lived there ourselves, at one time. If you are one of the millions who discovered the adventures of Calvin and Hobbes in the mid 1980s, you'll know how wonderfully Bill Watterson created a six-year-old's imaginary world, yet these comic-strip stories that took you to the planet Zorg and time-travelling in a cardboard box (among other things) were written for adults. At their peak, they were syndicated in 2,400 newspapers worldwide, and by the time *The Complete Calvin and Hobbes* was published, more than 30 million copies of the 17 books had been sold. *Something Under the Bed Is Drooling* was the title of one of them. Perhaps you remember when one of your children thought there could be monsters under the bed? If so, you probably found that commonsense and reasoning didn't work. To small children these monsters are real: a threat to life and limb.

Chaplain Larry Hirst, a Canadian Baptist pastor, who writes a *Chaplain's Corner* blog,[21] describes helping his two-year-old son over the fears. He found it was useless to try to convince his son that there were no monsters, so instead they prayed, and asked Jesus to keep them safe. They kept a night light on because monsters don't like the light, and kept the doors half open so that Dad could pounce on any monsters if they tried to sneak out even with the light on. Reverend Hirst had no intention to deceive or misguide. "I don't believe I was lying," he said, "I was simply entering into his world, his experience, his fears. I was letting him know that he was important, and that his feelings mattered to me. I was demonstrating to him that I was willing to do what could be done to insure his safety. It wasn't long until the monster ritual ended all on its own." Reverend Hirst was writing about the need to join the world of people with dementia.

Millions of parents step into their children's world at Christmas time, when they tell their children the story of Father Christmas. When it comes to Christmas, I have to confess I'm a purist. I think the story of Jesus' birth, with the Magi, the star and the shepherds is wonderful and amazing and absolutely enough in itself. But I do have the grace to keep my opinions to myself at Christmas time.

If parents are prepared to suspend their version of reality

so they can add sparkle to the world of a child for a short season, or to give comfort and reassurance, surely we can do the same for the well-being of a loved one with dementia.

Truth and grace

Even while understanding the benefits to the sufferer, people have raised objections on ethical grounds. Ms Coste tells of a woman who said, "How can I not tell my mother that her mother is dead? I can't do that to her." Ms Coste replied that she could, indeed, answer her mother's daily question in that way and continue to live with her mother's sobs and screams.

The real problem was that the mother was living in a past in which her mother was actually alive, and her daughter did not acknowledge it. How shocking to have someone tell you that a loved one you know and believe to be alive is actually dead! Think of the people who are dear to you and imagine how it would be if people around you kept insisting that they had died. The alternative, Ms Coste said, was to reply, "Oh, I'd love to see her too. She'll be here in about an hour. Let's have a cup of coffee while we're waiting for her." Anything to just get through the angst.

The problem is the emotion, not what the person is saying. When I say, "I want to see my mother," what am I saying? I'm saying, "I don't feel very safe."

"I'm not feeling safe" is usually the emotion behind the plea to go home, even when the person is in the home they've lived in for years. The person is looking for comfort, for assurance that all is well – that all will be well. "I want to go home" is heard often from dementia sufferers.

When the person with dementia is a Christian, and a

beloved husband or family member has died, it can be easier to handle. Roger's father died years before his mother, and when she had dementia she used to ask him, "When's Brian coming?" Roger would say, "Oh, he's waiting for us, you know. He's in heaven. Isn't heaven a wonderful place?" And he would go on to talk about heaven, his mother listening happily.

Behind every question is a plea for reassurance, and the caregiver's challenge is to find the answer that gives it. It would not be kind to force a widow to relive a bereavement each day. If she is living in an era where her husband was still alive, think of the likely places he could be when he isn't at home. Remember, it's not your world you're looking around – it's theirs. Once the person is reassured, you can move on – perhaps suggest having some hot chocolate, or a cup of tea.

A lady called Joy told me how her mother, who was looking straight at her, said, "I'll be glad when Joy is here. Where is she?" Without missing a beat, Joy burbled, "Well, let me see. It's a Thursday afternoon; let's see if we can remember what she does on a Thursday afternoon. School" – pause, "Girl Guides" – another pause, and on she went with random comments about Joy, hoping that one of them would hit the mark. She was trying to find which decade her mother was in at that moment, so she could have a reasonable answer about the whereabouts of the girl Joy. Her mother was happy to listen, as talking about Joy seemed to bring her presence into the room.

Coping with repetition

The same principle applies to repetitive questioning. Having to answer the same question again and again can be maddening. At one of our conferences a much-loved pastor and writer from South Wales, the Revd Geoff Thomas, spoke of his sense of failure when it came to responding to his mother's repeated questions.

Pastor Thomas's mother's family were of the Welsh Revival generation, rooted and grounded in Christ. She had been a typical Welsh "Mam" and he had been an only child. (You have to be Welsh. or perhaps Italian, to fully appreciate what that means.) He remembered, "Every chore my mother did, she accompanied with singing hymns under her breath, hardly knowing what she was doing." But in her seventies she had a series of "strokes", and developed vascular dementia. She became morose, and stopped singing hymns. The worst thing was the repetition. "She loved to go to meetings. She would go to meetings every night of the week, if there were any. And so at 5 o'clock, she began her questions. 'Is there a meeting tonight?' 'No, there's no meeting tonight, Mam.' And a few minutes later: 'Is there a meeting, then? Tonight?' 'No, there's no meeting tonight, Mam.' And then a few minutes later: 'Is there a meeting tonight?'

"And after this for half an hour, I would have to leave the room, fuming with anger and frustration, and annoyed with myself, and ashamed of myself. I am a man of God. I'm a preacher: I tell people how to live, how to cope in a fallen world. I tell them of their constant access to an indwelling Spirit. I tell them, 'Honour your father and your mother.' But after an hour of repetitive questions, and asking can she go home, and angry because she can't go home – 'I'm going home now, then. Take me home' – I get wound up. And hateful, and impatient. As mean as a ferret in a barrel. How little grace I showed. How angry I became!"

I've never seen a ferret in a barrel but it's hard to imagine this softly spoken pastor being like that, because he's among the mildest, most compassionate of men. But caregiving constantly, day in and day out, wears you down, and repetitive questioning can be like the drip, drip of the ancient Chinese water torture. Thank God, said Pastor Thomas, that "The blood of Jesus Christ cleanses us from all sin" (1 John 1:7 NKJV).

One of the three "commandments" of the SPECAL method is to learn to love repetition. That there might come a day when the person isn't able to communicate at all, is part of the thought. The solution could be in finding the right answer, the one that addresses the anxiety. Try listing possible answers on a sheet of paper, trying them out and then using the one which has the desired effect. One man tells of tuning out and responding half-heartedly to his wife's repeated question, until she asked the question again and said, "What did you say? What did you say?" Not remembering what he had said, he answered, "Only that I love you." Her face lit up with a big smile and that was the end of the repetition, for a while. It's finding the antidote to the emotion, not the answer to the question. "What time is my appointment with the doctor tomorrow?" asked repeatedly could mean, "I'm afraid I'll forget my appointment with the doctor tomorrow, because I know my memory is so bad!" The answer could be, "I won't let you forget the appointment, because I'm coming with you." As an aside, it's best not to tell the person about an appointment well in advance – just make sure they get there.

A common plea from sufferers is, "I want to go home." One care home in England has transformed its second floor into an indoor world, including a garden and a bus stop. The manager said that some people would keep saying that they wanted to go home and nothing could distract them. Now, when they want to go home, they can go and wait and sit on a bench at the bus stop. The aim is to stimulate conversation among the people waiting, as well as give them a sense of purpose. The answer to "I want to go home" could be, for a Christian, "We are going Home, dear; we're going all the way Home. Won't it be wonderful when we get there!"

POINTS TO PONDER

- If you are diverting someone from an activity, as Linda did with Frank and the flowers, give it a positive lift. Don't challenge, or put down.

- Jesus did not hold back from entering our world. He is the only one who can declare the end from the beginning, yet he lived with us in our timeframe and with all our misunderstanding as a result of the fall.

- Understand that behaviour which may be puzzling to you will have a meaning to the person with dementia, relating to something in their past.

- People with dementia often relate situations in the present to the past. They are not being delusional. Their world is as real as yours. Something that is true in your world may not be true in theirs, and the other way around, too.

- People with dementia experience high levels of anxiety. Many of their questions come from this feeling, rather than the words. Try several answers to see which one is the most effective.

- Learn to love repetition. Again, look to the emotion beneath the question, and try to find the answer that gives comfort and reassurance.

- Don't worry about giving the same answer again and again. The person won't notice the repetition, so it will be fresh every time to them. Once you've found the best

57

answer, use it. You are saved the strain of having to find a new one every time.

- When you feel guilty because of your imperfect reactions, remember that "The blood of Jesus Christ cleanses us from all sin." (1 John 1:7 NKJV)

Chapter 3

Could It Be Dementia?

Blessed are those whose strength is in you, who have set their hearts on pilgrimage. As they pass through the Valley of Baca, they make it a place of springs; the autumn rains also cover it with pools.

PSALM 84:5-6

"Simple test offers early dementia warning" was the headline that landed on my desktop with the press story. But what really caught my eye was a hyperlink with three blue words: "Dementia: Take the test".[22] The story was about a new test for dementia with ten tasks to assess mental abilities in "areas such as semantic knowledge, calculation, verbal fluency, spatial knowledge and mental recall." A study had found it could detect 93 per cent of patients with Alzheimer's disease, compared to the standard dementia test which accurately detected only 52 per cent. These days "Alzheimer's" and "dementia" are used almost interchangeably (although Alzheimer's accounts for most cases of dementia, there are numerous other causes), but I'm assuming that the test is for dementia, not exclusively for Alzheimer's. It has a good provenance, coming from Addenbrooke's Hospital in Cambridge and devised by consultant neurologist Jeremy Brown. The question for me was – should I do it, or not?

With a maximum score of 50 points, people with dementia tend to score around 33, and those with mild cognitive impairment (MCI) an average of 45. If there were questions on maths or shapes and sequences I would probably get the answer wrong and my score would be low. I'm one of those people who can't follow a map even when it's turned to face the way I'm going because the problem is, the map doesn't tell you where you are, exactly, at that moment. Whoever invented Sat Navs deserves a medal, in my opinion, although they do take a certain social element out of long journeys. Before Sat Navs I would make numerous stops to ask the way and to check where I happened to be, precisely, and as a result I met some very kind people and had many interesting conversations. Now I only have the crisp lady on the Sat Nav, who ignores me when I talk back to her. "Dementia: Take the test" would find me navigating on my own with no way of talking my way through it. What if the results said I had mild cognitive impairment? Absent-mindedness runs like a thread through my family, and mine could have become worse without my noticing. Although not all people with MCI go on to develop dementia, it is, as it says, an impairment, and it can become more serious: around 50 per cent go on to develop dementia. Juggling these thoughts and emotions, I was struck by how desperate people must feel when they have arrived at the point where they're asking themselves, "What's wrong with me? Could it be dementia?"

In reality, most people don't face the question posed as starkly or immediately, for the signs of dementia usually appear over a period of time and awareness that something is wrong dawns gradually. There are other conditions to consider, too, which can cause dementia but which can be treated, and once they have been cleared up the problems disappear. For example, elderly people are more prone to the side-effects of medications, and changing their prescription could be all that's needed. Some older people have found that taking Statins produces the symptoms of dementia; or it could be down to anaemia, a urinary infection, a thyroid disorder, or any number of other conditions. Depression in older people is sometimes referred to as a "pseudo-dementia", and here too, once treated, the signs of dementia disappear.

Among the early warning signs of Alzheimer's or dementia is not being able to smell your cup of morning coffee, or the roses in the garden. If you had a normal sense of smell all your life and you lose it, you may have a very early sign of Alzheimer's. "It has been known for some time that the brain regions first affected by Alzheimer's are the olfactory centres," said Dr Wilson, at Rush Alzheimer's Disease Centre.[23] Other, better known, warning signs are:

- Personal hygiene deteriorating: perhaps a stain on clothing the person does not notice, or forgetting to comb their hair every morning.
- Increasing memory loss for day-to-day activities, such as forgetting names of people, places or objects.
- Just not being able to recall something, and forgetting simple words, sometimes replacing them with less appropriate words.
- Disruption of normal routine without being aware of it.
- Disorientation in time and place, becoming lost and not knowing how to get home.
- Not wanting to get dressed and leave the house.
- Sleeping more than usual.
- Not taking care of their home as well as they normally did.
- Worsening judgment, such as dressing inappropriately for

the weather, or not seeking help for a serious problem.

- Losing abstract reasoning, such as understanding the significance of events or the ability to understand a principle.
- Misplacing things, even placing things in strange places, sometimes becoming paranoid or suspicious because they have disappeared, and suspecting that they have been stolen.
- Rapid mood swings for no apparent reason.
- Personality change, becoming apathetic, confused, suspicious or fearful.
- Loss of initiative, to the point where the person may not spontaneously engage in any activities.

Sometimes the symptoms can be masked by depression, as happened with Frank. He seemed to have lost his zest for life. It was this that first took Frank and Linda to the doctor and it was depression that he was initially treated for, with no thought of dementia. "It seemed to make sense that being redundant and having to leave a job you loved would make anyone depressed," said Linda. She has wondered since if the depression was the beginning of dementia; if perhaps his ability to do his job had already been affected and was making him depressed, and if it had contributed to him being asked to take early retirement. But at the time their friends and family agreed he was "down" because of the redundancy, and he would recover as time went on. And for a while the medication did seem to help. His mood lifted, although he rarely showed the same enthusiasm for anything as he had before. Then the worries began to escalate: "He began to forget things, and that would make him anxious. We've been going to the same church for years, and he'd say hello to people but wouldn't remember their names. Then it got so that sometimes he wouldn't remember the people themselves, either. There were other things, too. He was finding it hard to work things out. I got really worried when he began to get us lost driving home from church or from shopping. It was so unlike him. And I could see that it worried him, too, and he started to be more depressed again."

The changes in Frank were noticed more by their son, Matthew, who lived a few hundred miles away. He'd visit every other month, and on one occasion he made an excuse to take Linda into the kitchen to ask her, "What's going on with Dad? Does depression affect people like this? He's told me the same story, in exactly the same way three times today. And sometimes he isn't making sense. I can't put my finger on it, but he just doesn't seem to be himself."

They were puzzled and worried, but not thinking that it might be dementia because it was not as public then as it is today. Dementia has only appeared on the public radar in the last few years, and not always in the most helpful way. When media stories began to appear around five years ago, they were usually very negative with an emphasis on the last stage of the illness. Campaigning organizations profiled worst-case scenarios, as of course they must if they are to provoke change. One result is that for people over the age of fifty-five, the prospect of having dementia feels worse than anything else, including cancer. Many will avoid having a diagnosis, for that reason, pushing the possibility out of their minds. But, at that stage, Frank and Linda had no idea what could be causing the blanks in his memory and the occasional disorientation. None of their parents or older relatives had suffered with dementia.

It was when Frank became disorientated in his own living room that they knew something was radically wrong. Coming in from the garden early one evening, he asked Linda why she'd moved the furniture around. "Don't be daft! Why would I do that?" she replied. When he insisted, she said in exasperation, "If I'd moved the furniture you'd see scuff marks and light patches on the carpet, wouldn't you?" To her amazement, he got on his knees and began to check. Then she remembered their granddaughter's visit the week before, when they'd photographed her in her new dress standing in front of the patio doors. Linda had printed the photographs from the computer to put into their collection, and she fetched them and gave them to Frank. The furniture was in the same place. "I just hated to see the look in his eyes," Linda remembers. "He looked so frightened, and so lost. That's when we decided to go back to the doctor."

It's when we hear stories like this that my friends and I ask each other, "How do people manage to live, without Jesus?" How can they go through a crisis like this with only their own strength to draw on? It was to put a scriptural perspective into the dementia paradigm that *Could It Be Dementia? Losing Your Mind Doesn't Mean Losing Your Soul* was written. It's how we perceive things that gives them meaning, and sometimes we need reminding of what we already know. Our pilgrimage takes us through level plains, to ecstatic mountain tops and through some dry valleys, but we're promised springs in the valley of Baca – the valley of weeping (Psalm 84).

Dementia is an illness that happens mainly to older people; it comes on as we are nearing the end of our lives. But for those who have committed their lives to Christ, it isn't the end of everything and definitely not the end of us as individuals, because we know that the real life is yet to come. All of us from a certain generation know the phrase, "It's life, Jim, but not as we know it", made famous by Mr Spock as he reported to Captain Kirk about yet another strange planet from the bridge of the starship. We view our future from the bridge of Scripture through the telescope of the Holy Spirit. Some seem to see more clearly than others, especially those who are nearer the end of their pilgrimage, but we know that heaven is our destination and that we're nearer to it every day.

It's hard to explain to an unbeliever how deeply ingrained this "knowing" is in us. Perhaps you have to experience it to fully appreciate it. Ruth, a feisty 89-year-old who'd been a home manager in the days when managers were matrons, and had served on various committees for years after her official retirement, knew all about it. She was a typical pilgrim.

A trained nurse and midwife who'd worked in London during the Blitz, Ruth once ran the Society's largest home with around 100 residents, many in nursing care. When the building aged to the point where it was no longer viable, she oversaw their transfer to two other Pilgrim Homes.

It was a massive undertaking. Some were so frail that the doctor in charge told her many wouldn't survive the move, but Ruth enrolled all her prayer partners and her management and nursing skills, and there was not a single death for a full two years afterwards. Even in her eighties she stayed involved in different work for Pilgrim Homes, sitting on different committees, and providing the catering for some of the meetings in London.

She was also an active church member. Her pastor remembered, "We organized a charity pampering evening, to which any lady could come. To everyone's surprise, when we arrived, there in the car park waiting, was Ruth. She did everything – the head massage, manicure, pedicure – the lot, the whole time talking, making friends, building bridges over which she would seek to carry the good news of Jesus Christ."

Ruth lived life to the full. Given a diagnosis of cancer at the age of eighty-nine, Ruth knew she was nearing the end of her pilgrimage and she told her pastor, "Don't pray for me to get better, pray for me to go quickly!" To me she said, "Do you think we could be raptured soon? I'd rather go by air!"

She seemed to have an almost greater sense of where she was going than where she was, and was so looking forward to it. Sitting drinking tea in her flat, we promised each other that we'd meet there and worship together. Death really had lost its sting (1 Corinthians 15:55). In this, too, Ruth was a typical pilgrim.

Roger's mother was in hospital at a late stage in dementia, and he was asked by a nurse about the names his mother was repeating, barely audibly but determinedly. "Can you remember any of them?" he asked. She did, and he recognized his mother's prayer list. The closer she moved to heaven, the more it filled her horizon.

Diagnosis like a rugby tackle

Frank's visit to his doctor was the first of several. First he had a thorough physical examination to eliminate other causes. When he went back to talk over the results with his GP, the doctor asked more questions both of Frank and of Linda. Then she ran Frank through the MMSE (Mini Mental State Evaluation) and referred him to an Old Age Consultant at the local hospital. It was this Consultant who said she would like Frank to have a brain scan and afterwards, discussing the results, told them that Frank was suffering from dementia caused by vascular changes and Alzheimer's disease. "She was quite cold," Linda recalls. "She just told Frank that he'd have to give up his driving licence. Just like that. I thought it was hard."

"Having a diagnosis is like being rugby tackled," said one husband after they were told his wife had Alzheimer's. "Both of you hit the ground." Frank and Linda were left to pick themselves up and get on with their lives. But at least they felt they now knew what they were dealing with. In a sense, Frank felt relieved to know that there was a physical reason for what was happening.

But tens of thousands of people in the UK who are suffering with dementia have never been diagnosed, often because their symptoms are dismissed as an inevitable consequence of old age. In 2008 a national newspaper published a survey of family doctors about their dementia practice. 29 per cent said they had not had enough training to diagnose and manage dementia; 60 per cent were reluctant to give a diagnosis because there was no help they could offer, and 40 per cent were inhibited by the lack of effective drugs. The ruling that prevents the NHS prescribing specific drugs in the early stage of the illness still stands, although they can be purchased privately. Health board managers say the cost is prohibitive, but the reality is that it takes just a few weeks before it becomes clear if the patient is one of the 50 per cent for whom the drugs work.

Most worrying of all were the 10 per cent of GPs who said outright that as there was nothing that could be done for "victims", it was best not to diagnose at all. In one of Britain's largest cities, Birmingham, an estimated 82 per cent of sufferers were said to be undiagnosed. In America, research suggests that 65 per cent of people with Alzheimer's or other dementias are not diagnosed.

It was in response to findings like these that the British government announced a new national dementia strategy. Plans include training doctors to recognize the signs of dementia and ensuring that there is a memory clinic in every major town, where teams of doctors and nurses will provide help to patients and caregivers. Patients could be given behavioural therapy and memory strategies, or put on to special diets or exercise programmes and possibly be given memory-enhancing drugs. They would be allocated a key worker to guide them through the maze of help available from their local authority.

It all sounds very positive. The big question is whether or not there will be the money to back it. Speaking at a meeting in May, Professor Sube Banerjee,[24] the lead writer of the strategy document, said that for the plan to succeed, practitioners will need to push passionately for funding in their local areas. He said that although additional funding was available for local authorities, without a shared local vision the money would not reach dementia services. That sounds distracting as well as discouraging – it's hard to deliver services while at the same time having to fight for the funding.

Is it surprising that family doctors need training to spot the signs of dementia? Generations ago, they would be a part of the community they served, and would know individuals very well. Local practices would have one or two doctors and a manageable patient list. Today the average doctor's list is 2,000 patients. Information is held on computer and instantly available throughout the practice, but when the patient is seen, the doctor will be relying on a good summary left from a previous visit by another GP. It turns patients into "units of production"[25] and it cannot be satisfactory for highly educated doctors to have to work like this. "With all this technology there is a danger you can fail to see the woods for the trees," said Lord Winston, medical scientist and broadcaster. Speaking at a lecture, he said that although doctors' training emphasized communication, there is so much diagnostic technology available now that doctors are losing the ability to listen to the patient. Contact with the patient should remain "the essence of medicine", he said.

Knowing individuals personally is really the gold standard. My father was confined to bed for years because of a heart and chest condition which sometimes became acute, and I'm sure that had my mother not been a capable nurse, he would have died years before he did. I remember our GP striding through the door with his bag in his hand and, more often than not, warding off my mother and saying, "Don't tell me, please! Let me make my own diagnosis!" These days my father would have to go to A & E; he would possibly have to wait on a trolley in a corridor or an ambulance outside and then would eventually be seen by someone who knew neither him nor my mother. Still, the diagnosis would be relatively straightforward, relying on visible, physical symptoms. It is not so easy with dementia, which is why it is a process, and not a snap judgment. A doctor friend of mine once shared her concerns about her father, a former barrister, who had such good social skills that he could hide his mistakes and lapses, and I'm sure they would be missed for some time by a doctor who didn't know him.

Hopeful new signs

Now, with so much more attention being given to dementia, the signs are that people are being given more help. Said to be "blazing a trail in the early intervention and management of dementia",[26] and often cited as an example of best practice, is the Croydon Memory Service. People are referred to the Service by their GPs, and assessments are carried out by members of a small, multidisciplinary team led by clinical psychologist David Matthews. He agrees with other specialists that the earlier a diagnosis is made, the better. "It reduces the difficulties experienced by the client and their carer and the potential mental and psychological problems. If nothing else, it gives them more time to come to terms with the situation," he says.

Individuals are then visited at home by two members of the team who carry out an initial assessment. They also interview family members. The next step is an appointment at the Centre for other examinations, perhaps including a head scan and blood and urine screening. There will also be a care assessment and an occupational therapy assessment, looking at motor skills and processes. The team sees it as key to providing patients with a range of information so they can make informed choices and stay in control of their situation, and the team member who initially assessed the individual will continue as care coordinator. A range of medical and practical therapies are on offer. It's likely that only a few centres will have this level of excellence, but it provides a benchmark others are aiming for – and it is encouraging to see other local authorities announcing their intentions, too.

Alzheimer's can only be definitely diagnosed after death by examining the brain. But a quick summary of the process is: asking questions of you and your family; a physical examination; laboratory tests; cognitive tests (of different sorts, usually including the Mini Mental State Examination); and brain scans.

It's been suggested that people who are worried about their mental state should be able to refer themselves to a Memory Clinic. But opinion is divided over whether self-referral to Memory Clinics would improve diagnosis, or merely clog up the system with inappropriate cases. The British Psychological Society warned that trials had showed open referrals led to many inappropriate referrals being bounced back to GPs.

Denial can be dangerous

There are people who would rather not know. They who believe that, as there's no cure, it's best not to have a diagnosis because it would upset either them or the person with dementia unnecessarily. Family members will encourage loved ones to believe that these memory lapses and so on are just a normal part of growing old. There are a small number of people in our care homes who have never been given an official diagnosis because their family has avoided it. Hopefully, as the new approaches percolate through the system, the dread of dementia will be diluted, if not altogether removed, and this ostrich attitude will disappear.

One wife said, "After years of struggling with his progressive memory loss, I decided not to tell my husband that he was suffering from Alzheimer's. My children and I felt that because he was so far along he could not comprehend the fact that he was suffering from an incurable illness." A daughter explained that instead of upsetting their mother with specific details of her illness, she and her family members tell her not to worry, it must be old age. Sometimes relatives know in advance that the person does not want to know. "My wife made it clear that she did not wish to know if she had a serious illness," said a husband, "so when the diagnosis was made I chose to tell her that she had a slight memory problem. The truth would have upset her and would have gone against her wishes."

If the individual lives alone, as many older people do these days, denial can be downright dangerous. It's a paradox that although we have more wealth and experience to share than ever, most people seem to want to be by themselves. In the UK two thirds of people over the age of sixty-five are living on their own. Among the government's new dementia strategies should be a warning, for more and more studies are showing that where there is social isolation and people are not socially engaged, they have a higher risk of developing dementia. Yet our society seems to be becoming increasingly fragmented. Recently a newspaper carried a story about an elderly lady whose decomposing body was found in her apartment five years after she had died. Five years, and no one had missed her! Politicians spoke of their horror over the tragic case, which one described as "a glaring example of the country's fractured society".[27] Hers was an extreme case, perhaps, but similar stories are reported with increasing frequency. Only last week a carpenter told me he'd been called to repair a front door after the landlord had broken it to get in, because the tenant hadn't responded to telephone calls or letters. They found he'd been dead for three weeks.

Things that we take for granted become a challenge for older people. Balance can be a problem and in the early stages of dementia falls are not uncommon. So is a lack of concentration and forgetfulness. One of my most dramatic memories is of an older neighbour, who forgot that she had started to cook a meal. She walked away from a pan of cooking oil on her stove and it overheated and, in minutes, ruined most of her house. Fire and smoke swept through the kitchen and hallway, consuming a downstairs cloakroom before racing up the stairs. It was hard to tell which was the most shocking – the damage or the speed of the fire. Remembering to take medication is another problem, especially for someone with dementia. A mother with dementia said she wanted to stay in her own home for as long as possible, and her family did all they could to help her achieve this. They bought her two sets of pillboxes with compartments and marked them with the day of the week and "morning" and "evening". One was for their mother's home and one for a family member who would fill it and have it ready each week when their mother's ran out. They left little notes in strategic locations in her home to remind her to take her pills, and would telephone her every night and every morning. At first they assumed that all was well but they soon discovered that after they had called she would hang up and forget. Then they stayed on the line until she came back and confirmed that she had taken her pills. Eventually even that failed, and as they were living some distance away, they arranged for a carer to go in each day.

A central plank of the government's dementia strategy is keeping people in their own homes by providing greater support and more community-based services. Paradoxically, if it engenders more social isolation, with the known risk factors, it could lead to more cases of dementia. It is a tremendous opportunity for church fellowships to get involved. Six years ago Malcolm Goldsmith, a research fellow within the Dementia Services Development Centre at the University of Stirling and an ordained minister, wrote:

To face up to the presence of dementia within our midst is to discover opportunities for service and growth that are entirely consistent with the church's distinctive mission and role within society. To ignore that challenge is to raise serious questions, not only about our understanding of what it means to be a church, but also our understanding of what it means to be human. To ignore that challenge must raise questions about our understanding of the importance of the spiritual dimension to life and to the lives of countless people, many of whom would be included in "these, the least of my brethren" (Matthew 25:40).[28]

Points to Ponder

- Depression can mimic dementia. Don't ignore depression – see your doctor, who may prescribe medication or arrange for you to see a counsellor.
- Don't avoid a diagnosis, either for you or for your loved one. Ignoring it won't make it go away. Knowing what's wrong allows you to make plans and access the community care available.
- Diagnosis is a process. Much more is known about dementia now. And it may be that you have a different underlying condition that can be treated.
- Do share the diagnosis with your family and with your church leaders and those close to you.
- Stay socially connected. There will be challenges, but don't allow them to lead you into becoming isolated.
- Always remember that for Christians, this life is a pilgrimage. We are on a journey to somewhere unimaginably better – and the company is out of this world!
- Remember too, that the Holy Spirit has promised never to leave you.
- Mention to your pastor the importance of visiting older people who are living alone, especially if they are not coming to church as frequently as before.

Chapter 4

Honouring "Thou"

Be devoted to one another in brotherly love. Honour one another above yourselves.

Romans 12:10

Some months ago I bought my little granddaughter Lucy a cuddly toy that could talk. She sat it on the kitchen table to give it a thorough inspection. "It will talk to you if you squeeze its hand," I told her, so she leant over and took its hand in hers. "Hello, Princess," it said. Lucy gasped and her mouth became a big "O" of astonishment. "How did it know?" she asked. Although we always use her name, Lucy knows that she is the princess of our family here in Wales. Millions of other families around the world have their own princesses, of course, and we have two more in America. It's more than a term of endearment because it tells them they belong and are valued. It's a constant reinforcement that helps to build their self-esteem and sense of identity, both of which are essential for healthy relationships.

Our identity is the platform from which we view ourselves in relation to our families, our society, our gender and our beliefs. It's also about how we perceive and value each other, and of course, there's much more. At the root of many of the issues that bring people to counselling is a poor sense of identity. Ultimately, though, a believer's identity springs from a deeply personal relationship with the Father God.

Thanks to sophisticated technology, neurologists are discovering more and more about the brain and how it works. But they're no nearer to discovering the seat of the "self". In his column in the *Telegraph* on 9th February 2009 Dr James le Fanu wrote:

> The implications are clear enough: while theoretically it might be possible for neuroscientists to know everything about the physical structure of the brain, its "product", the mind, with its thoughts and ideas, impressions and emotions… still remain unaccounted for. "We seem as far from understanding the brain as we were a century ago," says the editor of Nature, John Maddox. "Nobody understands how decisions are made or how imagination is set free."

Scientists have recently discovered a functional system in the brain that they think may play a major part in reinforcing our memories and identity.[29] Dubbed "the default network", it uses more energy than nearly any other area of the brain, and it springs into action when the brain is either day-dreaming or in early sleep. It constantly chatters to the hippocampus, which records and recalls personal memories such as yesterday's breakfast or your first day of school. Researchers hypothesize that this default network reviews and evaluates our memories, giving us a kind of "inner rehearsal" for considering future actions and choices. Its activity is so important that it engages whenever possible, breaking off only when it has to divert its supply of blood, oxygen and glucose to a more urgent task. This important function is disrupted in a number of conditions, including depression and Alzheimer's. Without the reinforcing effect of the default network, we lose that sense of continuity in time between who we are and what experiences we have had: not only does our world become uncertain, but also our identity.

It might explain why people with dementia can seem to lose their sense of identity, and I stress *seem* to lose, because the essence of the person doesn't change, only their ability to make sense of themselves and their world. The effect is to make them behave differently, and out of character. "I wake up each morning and look over at Jack, and think how much I love him," said the wife of someone with dementia, "and then he wakes up and it's not Jack." It's why John Suchet says he's lost his wife, though she's still alive. It's what Nancy Reagan meant when she referred to "the long goodbye" of her husband's dementia.

Where the frontal lobes of the brain are affected, it can be particularly pronounced, as described earlier in Chapter 1. Thank God he always sees us as we are, because he looks on the heart. Nothing can hide us from him, including dementia.

It's easy to see why building the person up and helping to preserve their sense of identity is the most important aspect of dementia care. I remember watching a play in which the heroine was being subjected to psychological torture, part of which was to persuade her that she was someone else. She was kept in a room with distorting mirrors that altered her reflection, but she kept repeating to herself, "I am me, I am me, I am me." I've forgotten the rest of the story but not the horror of that particular scene. For if we're not who we believe ourselves to be – if we lose our identity – how could we imagine another, or how could we build another? The first book Christine Bryden wrote following her diagnosis had the poignant title, *Who Will I Be When I Die?* "I need you to be the Christ-light for me, to affirm my identity and walk alongside me… As I lose an identity in the world around me, which is so anxious to define me by what I do and say, rather than who I am, I can seek an identity by simply being me, a person created in the image of God", she said at a conference.

Dementia care is demanding and complex, so I asked one of our "front-liners", an experienced care home manager, "Would you say that reinforcing the person's identity is the most important aspect of dementia care?" She thought for a moment, then said definitely, "Yes, it is."

For believers, the Scriptures are strongly reaffirming. The Bible itself says that the Word of God is active and living, (Hebrews 4:12), and more than one of our care home managers have told me of the calming effect of Scripture readings and quoting Scripture verses. The Bible also links with strong memories from their past, particularly as many older people learnt to memorize Scripture verses in their Sunday school days.

Living by design

Jesus said that the second most important commandment was to love the person next to you as much as you do yourself (Mark 12:31). "Therefore encourage one another and build up one another, just as you also are doing," the apostle Paul told the Thessalonians (1 Thessalonians 5:11, NASB). What does it mean in practice? It's not arguing or insisting that the individual acknowledges your sense of reality. It means agreeing with the sense of situations as the person sees them, always emphasizing the positive and giving glowing praise. It's taking "the lower place" and saying "silly me" when there's been a misunderstanding or mistake.

God designed life to work, and for individuals to be built up through relationships with one another, and we are given a perfect example with God the Father, the Lord Jesus Christ and the Holy Spirit. It is interesting to see how the Designer's principles govern everything in life, whether they are acknowledged or not. A study of over 5,000 people found that Alzheimer's patients who have a close relationship with their caregivers show a slower decline in their mental and physical function over time.[30]

I and Thou was the title of a landmark book by the Jewish philosopher Martin Buber some years ago. It influenced many psychologists, including Tom Kitwood, the trailblazer in dementia care. Buber asserted that relationship is primary in life, and that the essence of relationship is the "I–Thou" mode that acknowledges the sacred nature of God. Much of his thesis falls outside Christian exegesis, but in acknowledging that humans are made in God's image, he was on the right track. Perhaps this sense of the sacred is why many Christians still use "Thou" in prayer. "Thou" has a warmth and intensely personal focus that makes "You" seem quite utilitarian. The famous hymns, "Thine Be the Glory" and "How Great Thou Art" would not sound the same using "You". "Thou" was used in Yorkshire until fairly recently for close friends and family and is retained in some of their old sayings.

No one is suggesting that "thou" should be used with individuals with dementia (even people in Yorkshire would regard you warily if you made that suggestion!), but the characteristics should be there. Individuals are to be "honoured": they have been made in God's own image. It's worth looking at this a little more closely, because it helps to explain how care that honours the "thou" could help preserve the individual's personality.

Tom Kitwood's view was that "all events in human interaction – great and small – have their counterpart at a neurological level". He argues that a "malignant social psychology" – that is, derogatory treatment of an individual, based on stigmatisation and ageism – has a profoundly negative effect that can lead to nerve-tissue damage, whereas Buber's "I–Thou" relating that honours the individual has a positive response that "may correspond to a biochemical environment that is particularly conducive to nerve growth."[31]

There seems to be growing attention to the neuroplasticity of the brain, and the way its physical structure changes as it responds to learning. In his book, *The Brain That Changes Itself*, psychiatrist Norman Doidge argues that because the brain is malleable, it can change its own structure and replace lost functions.[32] Conversely, poor care, such as treating the person indifferently or as an object, could lead to further damage.[33]

Dr Habib Chaudhury, an expert in old age and dementia at Simon Fraser University, Canada, has recently published a book called *Remembering Home: Rediscovering the Self in Dementia*.[34]Although his book is written for experts like himself (it mentions things like "periaqueductal gray matter-hypothalamic-limbic regions"), he is looking at ways of helping people recapture themselves. He suggests Reminiscence Therapy, particularly by revisiting past experiences that have positive emotional attachments.

Reminiscence Therapy can work powerfully because it takes the person back to memories they still retain, helping them to regain their sense of self. After many years of marriage, Linda knows her husband very well. She has shared many of his experiences and knows which ones to tap into, and she does it instinctively. Thinking of their lives in terms of a photo album, Linda knows the right pages to turn to; pages with photographs of events that were significant and gave him the most pleasure. They would also be a reminder to him of who he is.

Life pictures and traffic lights

The concept of a photo album is a good way of explaining how our memories work, with the earliest memories at the bottom, and the latest at the top. "Using our album is as fundamental to our mental existence, as breathing is to our physical existence," said Oliver James. "We take it for granted, it happens automatically and it is a critical component of our identity. It enables us to know what's what at every waking moment."[35]

Imagine that you are not able to remember recent events. You can't store any new photos with facts, only feelings. If you are challenged, or asked a question about something you did five minutes ago, you will find yourself staring into nothingness – into an empty photo frame. You will not be able to remember the unsettling experience you had half an hour ago, but you will remember the feelings, and they will be associated with the people or the place involved. Simply finding blanks is frightening. The SPECAL organization offers carers "Photo Album training", because it not only explains how individuals can only make sense of the present in the light of the past, but also why it's important to avoid the "red danger" state of terror when confronted with a blank photo.

Imagine it happening to you. You drive to your bank to deposit a cheque for a sizeable amount, rather than put it through the post. When you get to the counter you can't find the cheque, even though you look thoroughly through your handbag. Upset over the loss, you drive home and find your bank books where you'd left them and, flicking through the paying-in book, you see that you'd paid the cheque in the day before. You telephone your daughter and ask if you can use her tumble dryer because it's raining, then she reminds you that you have one of your own. You're asked to post a letter and you put it carefully in your handbag, but forget all about it. When you're asked if you posted the letter you say, "What letter?" and your friend points out that you put it in your bag. You open your bag and there it is, but you have no memory of either being asked to post it or putting it there.

Good care wants to build up with love, not knock down with fear. The aim is to keep the person in a state of contentment, and there are three states of mind to watch. SPECAL colour codes them like traffic lights. Green is good, as it means the person is contented; amber is a warning that green has been lost and red is looming, and red is for danger – to be avoided and moved out of quickly. Frank had moved into amber when he wanted to drive the car, but Linda quickly turned him to green when she reminded him that he said he'd sit next to her to give her confidence, as he was such a good driver. In one small sentence she also affirmed his identity and worth. She also helped to keep him in green and didn't argue that it was the wrong driveway when he directed her into their neighbours'.

In our relationships we're generally good at mood control, and we can usually tell what someone is feeling. My husband used to have a particular way of shrugging his shoulders when he was annoyed, and an entirely different shrug of the shoulders when he was saying that something was good. I used to think that when I disagreed strongly with someone my expression was inscrutable, but someone told me that "stony-faced" is a better description.

Keeping Frank on green is part of Linda's "Italian Traffic Conductor" role, as she tries to avoid situations that would send him into amber or red zones. She's grateful that, as well as their family photographs, many of the "feel-good" photographs in their lives are about things to do with their Christian fellowship, and there is so much to draw on: the summer barbecues, the mid-week meetings, the baptisms and other special events. It was so much more than just going to church on Sunday, although that had never been just a duty and was as central to their lives as breathing. Simply being there did them good, Frank used to say, whatever the sermon was like. He'd been a bit disgruntled a few years back when some of the old hymns had been pushed to one side and some new songs introduced, but eventually a balance had been struck and now they had a mixture of old and new. Some innovations he thought were a very good idea, like the big projection screen that meant you didn't have to keep your head down on the hymn book, though he'd joked that it might have been better if he had, because he sang like a rusty crow.

A couple of years ago he began to need the toilet more frequently, and at the same time started having trouble fastening his clothes, and because of this they'd stopped going to church. Linda could help him at home but not in the men's toilets at church. They thought they'd listen to taped sermons at home on a Sunday, but one of their friends came around and asked what was wrong. It was a difficult moment because Frank was embarrassed and clearly in an amber zone, but his friend made light of it and said he'd sit next to him at the back of the church and go with him to the toilet when he needed. "You've been going to church for how many years?" he said jocularly. "You're not going to let a little thing like that stop you now, are you?" Frank saw the funny side, and the two couples made sure they sat regularly together at the back of the church. A bonus for Frank was that when he was not so anxious about the toilet, he rarely needed it in church. Sometimes people with dementia can be very disruptive in church, but Frank sits contentedly.

"Most churches can cope with a disruptive infant or child in church, but not someone with dementia," Roger comments. Perhaps a more relaxed attitude will come with more experience, and clearly, as numbers increase, churches are going to have to learn how to cope with members with dementia.

A daughter, who was her father's main caregiver, told how she'd tried a couple of churches in her area, looking for one that would accept him and where he would feel comfortable. Eventually she found one that seemed to fit the bill. Everything went well until the pastor mentioned that believers were only temporarily in the world and were all going Home, at which point her father shouted out loudly, "Home, Home on the Range!" Instead of there being a moment of acute embarrassment, the pastor stopped and said, "Yes, that's it! We'll all be Home on the Range. Why don't we sing that? Musicians, do you know how to play it?" And everyone stood and sang "Home on the Range", to the delight of her father. How many churches could be that spontaneous, I wonder? Are we made more holy by an inflexible, predictably structured service each Sunday? Does it help us focus on the ultimate "Thou", or is it simply scaffolding that is more psychological than spiritual?

When the pastor led the church in singing "Home on the Range", first and foremost he was honouring the "Thou". He was also releasing a strongly therapeutic touch, for music has surprising properties. In the Bible we read how David played the harp to ease King Saul's depression. And the army of King Jehoshaphat intimidated the huge army advancing from Edom when the musicians and dancers went out in front of the soldiers. They weren't doing a version of the New Zealand All Blacks' Haka war dance, either, but they were singing, "Give thanks to the Lord, for his love endures forever" (2 Chronicles 20:21). It was a highly unusual strategy but it worked.

When Linda was looking for a way of helping Frank feel less anxious when they shared the housework, their pastor suggested that she play some Christian music in the background. Frank had never been particularly musical so she didn't really think it would help, but anything was worth a try. So before getting out the vacuum cleaner and dusters the next time, she showed him the CD and said that they were going to have a sort of *Music While You Work* time. *Music While You Work* had been the title of a radio programme from their parents' era, and they both remembered it from their childhoods. To her surprise, Frank began humming to the music and his mood seemed to lighten. He still moved things about and put some in the rubbish bin, and the furniture continued its carousel when she was out of the room, but he seemed less anxious – which in turn made her feel more at ease, too. Playing Christian music became a backdrop to the housework and gradually extended to other parts of their lives, and she wished she'd thought of it before. She found some CDs of the "old" music he'd liked and she's surprised at how well he remembers some of the lyrics.

Music therapy is prescribed for people with high levels of stress. It's been found to reduce pain during dental and even some surgical procedures. Music was played when Fran, one of our reviewers, had an operation on her foot under local anaesthetic. It was partly to cover the sound of the operation and partly to calm the patient, she was told. In counselling, music is often played at the beginning of a session to create a relaxed atmosphere. Even playing music in the background while we are working, seemingly unaware of it, has been found to reduce stress and anxiety. Neither Linda nor Frank had good singing voices. But she'd never really minded what they sounded like. They'd always enjoyed worshipping at church and that's what mattered. "We'll sound like angels in heaven," she told herself as she pottered last thing at night, and wondered what sort of instruments they'd have to play. But it was the thought of her and Frank being together, perfectly whole, that lifted her spirit the most.

POINTS TO PONDER

- Reinforcing the identity of the person with dementia is at the heart of dementia care. They need constant affirmation of their worth – even if it seems to be "over the top" with an adult.

- Honouring the divine image of each human being, particularly when a person has dementia, can help produce physical, positive changes in the brain. It will not lead to a cure – but it may help delay the progression of the disease. It will certainly increase a sense of well-being, and help lift depression.

- Relationships are God's plan for human beings. We should be careful to nurture them throughout our lives, especially when an individual has dementia.

- Think of our memories of life events in the form of a photograph album. The photographs are stored with facts and emotions. Individuals with dementia are unable to store photos of recent events, but they will retain the feelings.

- Finding a "blank" photograph – that is, one with no facts – is frightening. Try to avoid situations where this might happen.
- Don't argue or try to reason with the person – it's better that they think *you* have made the mistake if there is a misperception, not them.
- Keeping the individual contented and in the green zone may help the brain "rewire".
- Finding someone to "befriend" at church may help the person with dementia feel more comfortable.
- Music has therapeutic properties. Try playing old favourites.

Chapter 5

Dealing with the Diagnosis

Since you are my rock and my fortress,
for the sake of your name lead and guide me.

PSALM 31:3 (NIV)

"How many kinds of sweet flowers grow in an English country garden?" begins an old English folk song. It's always been one of Frank's favourites and he used to sing it to his grandchildren sometimes. "We'll tell you now of some that we know, those we miss you'll surely pardon. Daffodils, heart's ease and phlox, meadowsweet and lady smocks, gentian, lupin and tall hollyhocks, roses, foxgloves, snowdrops, forget-me-nots, in an English country garden."

Frank and Linda were in their garden doing some weeding one August afternoon when out of their neighbour's back door danced five-year-old Jenny, ahead of her grandmother, Sarah. "Hello!" said the sociable Jenny, going up to the fence and holding up a foot. "I've got new shoes, look!" Sarah explained that Jenny had just begun dancing class and was very taken with her new shoes. "They're very pretty shoes!" said Linda, and Frank beamed in agreement. He began to sing the old folk song, clapping his hands and shuffling his feet to its catchy rhythm, and Jenny joined in, dancing happily in her five-year-old way on her side of the fence. Sarah and Linda caught each other's eyes, smiling. Linda thought how far they'd come since the day when they'd come home from the specialist who'd told them that Frank had dementia. Here they were today, enjoying the late afternoon sunshine, with Frank singing and dancing, yet just over seven years ago she'd felt that they had been plunged into deep darkness. She wished that someone had told them that there is life after diagnosis, that the slide isn't always steep and swift and that there can be years ahead. And even when the person seems to be slipping away as the dementia develops, there will be moments like this when he will reappear as himself again, if only for a moment.

The day when life became AD – After Dementia – stood in her memory like an old tombstone. They hadn't been able to take it all in at once: the diagnosis is given at a point in time, but it takes a while for the full impact to roll out. They felt they were caught up in a kaleidoscope of emotions, each twist bringing a different set to the surface. There was bewilderment, anger, anxiety, guilt, grief, hope (that a cure might be found sooner rather than later), and for Linda, a growing sense of bereavement. It was as if the pattern of their lives had been etched in glass and someone had taken the glass and shattered it. Linda reckons it was months before they worked things through and reached a plateau where they felt balanced once more.

People react differently. "I felt totally alone, with the world receding from me in every direction and you could have used my anger to weld steel," said the author Terry Pratchett. Others feel shock, disbelief or total numbness. "I was very relieved to know that my problems were not imagined," a 63-year-old lady told my colleague, Janet, at a conference. "I feel liberated, and now I'm going to get on with my life. I have a list of things I want to do and I'm determined to live as fully as I can." She and her husband were both smiling as they talked to Janet. They had accepted what was happening and had planned together how to deal with it. They were lifelong believers, and had learnt how to take the long view, knowing that the best is yet to come. They believed the apostle Paul when he said:

> *For while we are in this tent, we groan and are burdened, because we do not wish to be unclothed but to be clothed with our heavenly dwelling, so that what is mortal may be swallowed up by life. Now it is God who has made us for this very purpose and has given us the Spirit as a deposit, guaranteeing what is to come.*

2 CORINTHIANS 5:4–6

Another word for "deposit" is "down-payment", and a down-payment is something that you have already been given. In giving us his Holy Spirit, God has given us a taste of glory, and he not only keeps us now but draws us towards heaven.

In contrast, another delegate, also in her sixties, said she was still in shock from the diagnosis. She and her husband were despondent. "We're not that old," he said. Their whole demeanour was one of defeat. They seemed to lack the resilience of the other couple. "I'm glad I was able to chat with them and encourage them," said Janet. Resilience is important and something we need to build, for the Bible tells us that people of faith can expect to go through many trials and tribulations. When things are going well it's easy to float along on the surface of life, but that doesn't anchor us properly in the Rock. We build resilience by constantly practising the things we believe. "Whatever you have learned or received or heard from me, or seen in me – put it into practice," wrote Paul to the Philippians. "And the God of peace will be with you"(Philippians 4:9).

Frank and Linda had always said, when asked, that they were "practising Christians". "We have to keep practising because we're far from perfect," Frank used to joke. Linda thinks it is because they are by nature very practical people, so their faith had never been merely theoretical. On hearing the diagnosis, Frank said that, among other things, he felt a sense of relief. "It's a physical illness," he said to Linda. "At least now we know the road we're going down." When life had seemed uncertain in the past, he used to quote one of his favourite verses from Psalm 138, and it came instinctively to him now: "The Lord will fulfil his purpose for me; your love, O Lord, endures forever – do not abandon the works of your hands." It seemed more relevant than ever, especially the psalmist's plea not to be abandoned.

Abandoned

A feeling of being abandoned is not unusual for people with dementia and their families. Often, the person has been behaving "oddly" for some time and others, not knowing what is happening, will have no idea how to cope. At times Frank seemed to "blank" people, but when he did join in a conversation he often repeated himself. He thought that people crossed to the other side of the street to avoid him, or moved away from him in church, though Linda wasn't so sure. Their close friends had put it down to Frank's depression, and they'd tried to cheer him up. Yet the truth is that we do avoid people with dementia, partly because it's outside our experience and we don't know how to communicate with them, and partly because we find it frightening.

A survey by the Alzheimer's Society in 2009 showed a

"shocking lack of understanding" in the UK when it comes to dementia. More than a third of the people surveyed mistakenly thought that it was a "natural part of ageing". The saddest thing for Christians is that this misunderstanding is also common in their churches, and when individuals and their carers find they're no longer able to go to church, they are allowed to gradually drift away – a tragic example of "out of sight, out of mind".

This was brought home to Roger when he was Director of Age Concern in Birmingham and running the largest day centre in the UK for people with dementia. He said, "As part of my normal work I visited a lady who was looking after her mother, who had very severe Alzheimer's. Her mother's behaviour had become so demanding that she needed support. As we discussed the situation she explained that because of her mother's distressing behaviour at times, all her friends had stopped visiting. Although she was a long-term member of a large and very active church, neither the pastor nor any member had been to see her for almost two years. At the close of our conversation I simply offered to read and pray with her (something I did not usually do then, because I was working for a secular organization). I read Psalm 41, and as I did she began to weep. She asked me who the Psalm was about. I showed her that it spoke of the Lord in his last days (verse 9) and his experience of distress, desertion and isolation. 'But that is Mum's and my experience,' she said. 'Does that mean that Jesus knows how I feel when I think of the condition that has afflicted Mum and me, and the way people have let me down?' I agreed, and just explained a little more how deeply the Saviour feels our distress and sorrow. Her smile of relief and even joy was amazing. She saw the 'fellowship of sharing his sufferings'."[36]

Some Psalms graphically express this particular aspect of dementia. Psalm 31:9–13 says:

Be merciful to me, O Lord, for I am in distress; my eyes grow weak with sorrow, my soul and my body with grief. My life is consumed by anguish and my years by groaning; my strength fails because of my affliction, and my bones grow weak. Because of all my enemies, I am the utter contempt of my neighbours; I am a dread to my friends – those who see me on the street flee from me. I am forgotten by them as though I were dead; I have become like broken pottery. For I hear the slander of many; there is terror on every side; they conspire against me and plot to take my life.

How dreadful that a damaged brain can make someone feel like this! Jesus knew the pain of being misunderstood, and of loneliness. Paul says in 2 Corinthians 1:5, "as the sufferings of Christ flow over into our lives, so also through Christ our comfort overflows." Roger, now a pastor, says, "Sometimes all you can do is to hold the person's hand, speak respectfully and show affection. Sometimes you will weep with a daughter, a husband, a son... it's not a bad thing, it's a part of caring."

Weeping with those who weep

Coming to terms with dementia is not instant, and it's not easy. At times Linda and Frank felt almost overwhelmed. How could this be happening to them? When they moved house some years ago they'd taken their lawyers' advice and made their wills at the same time. They'd discussed the possibility of one of them dying before the other but they'd never considered a long-term illness. Most of us don't. Yet now they were having to face dementia. How to tell their children and other family members? How would it affect their grandchildren? How to tell their friends? Some people keep the diagnosis to themselves for an extraordinarily long time, usually because they're not able to deal with others' reactions until they've worked through their own. "We were just about holding ourselves together," Linda remembers, "and we didn't know how we could cope with the children." They decided to ask their pastor to come round and pray with them, before they shared it with anybody else.

Harry had been pastor of their church for eleven years, and with something like 100 members, he knew most families fairly well. He knew that Frank had been struggling with depression and had prayed for him from time to time, but he was stunned to hear about the dementia. Linda's phone call came in the same week he'd taken the funeral of a sixteen-year-old boy who'd died suddenly from meningitis. The father was a friend of his and their families were close, so he came with a reservoir of sadness. Linda and Frank told him about Frank's diagnosis, haltingly at first, and then Linda's resolve to be sensible melted and she started to cry. Tears welled in Frank's eyes, and looking at them both, the dam broke in Harry and he could only sit speechless, his eyes also full of tears. When he found his voice, he put his arm round Frank's shoulder and said, "It is terrible, it's a dreadful thing." They simply sat and shared their grief for a while, before moving on to any discussion.

Linda said afterwards, "It was the best thing he could have done. I didn't want any advice or anything else right then, I just wanted us to be understood." Harry read from Psalm 31, saying that in writing it King David had poured out his soul at a desperately difficult time. Even so, he knew that he was held firmly in God's hand and could say, as Jesus did on the cross centuries later, "Into your hand I commit my spirit."

"We are pilgrims on our way to the new heaven and the new earth," Harry reminded them. But he said, too, that they needed to grieve. They might feel angry – and that was all right, too. "It's a grievous thing, it's not going to be easy, but we'll go through it together," he told them. When it came to telling the children and family, he advised them to do it sooner, rather than later, and to tell them as much as they knew, not trying to protect them by holding anything back.

Telling the family

There is no right or standard way of telling family and friends about a diagnosis of dementia, and much depends on the strength of the relationships and the personalities involved. Frank and Linda were worried most of all about their grandchildren. Frank takes a delight in his grandchildren, especially eight-year-old Benji, who shares his love of all things mechanical that have engines and wheels or wings. Children, especially young ones, seem to share a particular wavelength with the elderly and have a special rapport, as we saw earlier with Jenny and her dancing shoes.

Unlike adults, who will ignore embarrassing behaviour until it affects them personally, children will ask quite quickly what is wrong. The key is openness, being ready to answer questions at any time, say the experts. Children should be encouraged to ask questions and given simple and honest answers, without "sugar-coating" the message. Teach them as much as you can about the condition, and reassure them that, just because a family member has dementia, it does not mean that they or anyone else in the family is going to get it, too.

It's not infectious. Changes in someone with dementia, such as memory losses, are small at first and children will adapt to them. Forgetfulness, in small ways, is something everyone experiences, but when it is accompanied by strange behaviour, then problems can begin.

Even then, children can be very forgiving of grandparents. Prepare them for change, knowing the condition will get worse over time. This can be very hard for them, because the grandparent may look physically well and just the same as he or she always has, but they need to understand that, although the individual may look fine on the outside, on the inside their brain is not working as it should. Benji understood his Granddad's dementia from the concept of an engine that was not working properly. "Can't the doctor put something in there that would fix it?" he asked.

As the dementia progresses children can feel bewildered and anxious because they don't understand what is happening: there is sadness, because the beloved grandparent is changing; frustration, because of having to repeat things when they are not being understood; then guilt for getting angry; and they feel unsettled, because they are not sure how to behave around the grandparent. When we are children we feel that everything devolves on us, and that even our thoughts have power. They need to know that it's not their fault, to be helped to understand that people with dementia have good days and bad days, like the rest of us – but that they are not responsible, themselves, for the bad days.

Frank's son, Matthew, took the news stoically, though he was clearly upset. He wasn't altogether surprised, because he had noticed his father's memory lapses, and the way he would repeat things. Like his father and his nephew Benji, Matthew was practically minded and wanted to know if there were drugs or any other treatments that could help. He told his parents that he would do anything he could to help them. "Let me know what you need, don't fret about anything," he said. He was the first to download information through the internet.

Their daughter Kate reacted differently. She was clearly shocked by the diagnosis, but questioned whether it was accurate. "How could they tell for sure?" she wanted to know, and turning to Linda, asked why her father couldn't just get a grip of himself. Linda feels that Kate never really accepted the reality of her father's diagnosis. She visited less and less often, and was always on edge in his presence.

When faced with overwhelming emotions, one of our defence mechanisms is to deny them and to push them down. But if we don't face them they will not go away. Consigned to the basement, they will grow stronger and pervasive, affecting all our perceptions and our thinking. There is danger in denial, as already mentioned. Roger's mother struggled to come to terms with her diagnosis of dementia. "She just wouldn't grieve and accept that it was happening," he remembers. "She kept on trying to overcome it and to be cheerful. There were two years of turmoil. We do need to grieve."

Their friends were not surprised by the diagnosis. Although they had put Frank's "oddness" down to depression at first, they'd noticed the changes in him and, because they were all about the same age, they hadn't put it down to "just growing older". Their first question was, "What can be done about it?" Then, "What can we do?"

Benji seemed to grow closer to his grandfather over time, and Matthew grew more protective. Even towards the end of Frank's illness, when he seemed to be totally withdrawn and unable to talk, his face would light up when he heard Benji's voice outside his bedroom door. Frank eventually went to live permanently in a care home and although Benji was a teenager by that time, he would shout as he knocked on the door, "Coming in, Granddad!" (Incidentally, experts say that from the very beginning you should have in mind that you will need to plan for short periods of respite care to give the caregiver a break, and that in most cases, a nursing or care home will be essential for the well-being of both the sufferer and the caregiver towards the end.) And, until he went into the care home, whenever Frank was in the garden and saw the little girl who was visiting next door, he would smile at her, and she would chatter to him about inconsequential things that seemed to please them both. Even though Frank found it harder to communicate with words, they always seemed to understand each other.

POINTS TO PONDER

- Remember that there is life after a diagnosis of dementia. Though each person is different and timescales vary widely, the average length of the first stage is four to five years, the second stage three or four, and the final stage can be as short as a few months. But each individual is different, and the timings vary widely, from a few years to twenty. Generally speaking, the older the person is at diagnosis, the shorter the timescale.

- Pray with your pastor or church leader as soon as possible after the diagnosis. A burden shared is a burden less heavy. Don't be shy about asking for help – and ask about the best way of getting it, when you need it.

- Share the diagnosis. Keeping it to yourself is unproductive, not only for yourself but for others with dementia. You may not be like Terry Pratchett, sharing widely, but everyone that "names the demon" diminishes it a bit more.

- When someone shares a diagnosis of dementia with you, share the person's grief. Listen actively. Don't go into advice-giving mode. Don't ask, "Is there anything I can do?" Ask instead, "What can I do to help?" Make it clear that you'll be alongside for the duration, if you can.

- Small children and "seniors" often have a rapport. But for grandchildren and others in the family, do explain what is happening to Grandma or Granddad. Make sure they understand that it's nothing they've done – it's not their fault.

- Dementia brings high anxiety, especially in the early stages. Don't ignore people you know who have developed dementia. Ask their main caregiver the best way of communicating.

- Psalm 31 is a great comfort to Christians with dementia and their carers.

- Make a plan together, as far as you're able.

- Start to list useful information about respite care and eventual residential or nursing home care.

- Build resilience! Follow the Apostle Paul's advice. Even without dementia, old age has been described as the last battle. If you find yourself suffering with depression, see your doctor, or find a good Christian counsellor.

- Ask your pastor if there are people in your fellowship with dementia, perhaps not able to come to church now, that you could pray for.

Chapter 6

Practical Steps

Therefore put on the full armour of God, so that when the day of evil comes, you may be able to stand your ground, and after you have done everything, to stand.

If the new Memory Clinics work as planned, at the point of diagnosis people like Frank and Linda will be given heaps of information and support. They will even have a key worker who will guide them through the maze of social services, if they need it. But in those days Frank and Linda felt they only had each other. "The shock makes you feel very alone, very isolated," Linda recalls. "Even though we have family and friends, it throws you into yourself."

Living with dementia reminds me of the way businesses came through the recession in the 1990s. The managing director of one company, now immensely successful, says he learnt his best negotiating skills in keeping out the bailiffs. There were avalanches of advice for businesses in those days, with the Department of Trade and Industry and the Chartered Institute of Marketing releasing press stories nearly every week. But for many small-to-medium businesses, and some large ones too, success was summed up in three short words (four, if you count "We're" as two words). When asked, "How are you doing?" they would say, "We're still here." Though most didn't realize it, they were practising the biblical principle which says that you do all you can, and then, "having done all, to stand" (Ephesians 6:13 NKJV). For Christians, that means committing the situation to God, planning and taking all the practical steps possible, and then – just standing. In tackling dementia, there are three key things to consider, and they are:

(a)   The practical aspects, from the simplest, such as non-slip surfaces in the home, to the latest technical devices that will tell you, for example, when someone has been too long in the bathroom and may be in trouble.

(b)   The best treatment for sufferers, at the core of which is helping them to maintain their "personhood" – their unique, individual personalities.

(c)   Support and care for the caregiver – making sure that this key individual is supported by others, has whatever aids are available to help, and can take breaks. Too many caregivers feel like Atlas, carrying the world on their shoulders without a Hercules to hand it over to for a little while.

There is much excellent information on the Alzheimer's Society website,[37] including an encouraging quote from a workshop organized in Australia by Christine Bryden and Morris Friedell, a fellow campaigner working to give voice to people with dementia. They said, "Though you may need to build a whole new life in the slow lane, you don't need to be resigned to inevitable decline, lack of empathy and judgement. You can be a full participant in life – there are many options and possibilities ahead for you." Both went on to speak at other conferences and also wrote articles and books. Though Frank and Linda didn't know about the Alzheimer's website then, and hadn't been given any information, they applied much of it instinctively anyway because, as Linda says, "It's basically down-to-earth common sense."

Frank and Linda decided they would both keep as positive an outlook as possible, something Linda had become quite expert at doing to counterbalance the depression that had dogged Frank for the previous year or so. It's often as hard to live with a person who has depression as it is to be the person suffering with it. In an international survey conducted by the European Union a couple of years ago, depression came out as the "worst" of all health conditions. It's not surprising that the Bible tells us, "Above all else, guard your heart, for it is the wellspring of life" (Proverbs 4:23).

Frank's depression was already being treated with medication, but they knew that if they were to get on their feet again after their "rugby tackle", they would have to be determined about staying positive. They looked for things that would help. One of them was Frank's sense of humour and they decided they would make the most of that. They would watch light-hearted or uplifting DVDs and TV programmes, and they would look for the funny side of things as much as they could. Frank would sometimes fumble with the razor and flannel when he was shaving, but wanted to stay with the "wet" shave as long as he could. Looking at the results one morning, Linda said, "Any more scrapes and you'll look like Frankenstein!" "Not a good-looking lad like me," Frank laughed. In his early stages Frank was able to gather his thoughts and express himself quite well; though after a few years he began to have trouble with both. Linda resolved that they would take life quietly, one day at a time, and avoid any pressure, such as meeting commitments or having to rush.

They also made a "to-do" list, which looked something like this:

- Frank would consider himself cosseted; doing what he enjoyed and did best, leaving the rest to others. An example was stacking the dishwasher. He wouldn't need to do that any more because he was finding it hard to fit the plates into the racks. It was a bit like buttoning his shirt, where he couldn't get the button to go through the hole. Linda said it was easier for her because she was shorter than Frank and didn't have to bend down so far.

- Linda made a silent decision to boost Frank's confidence at every turn. Their daughter, Kate, had been a shy, anxious little girl and they used to accentuate her achievements in an almost exaggerated way, something they hadn't needed to do with their bouncy, extrovert son. Now, sensing Frank's growing lack of self-esteem, she made a mental note to do it whenever she could.

- They would decide how best to tell the children, and the grandchildren. First, they would get all the information they could from their doctor.

- When they were with people, such as their "home group", they would tell them about Frank's diagnosis, which would explain why he needed to be told things more than once, and might not seem to be taking things in.

- They would get one of the big calendar-clocks they'd seen in the market that showed the day and the date as well as the time, and put it in the sitting-room on top of the television where it would be very obvious.

- They'd put a big pin-board on a wall in the kitchen, and pin up important appointments or notes. They found a weekly schedule message board, and put that up too.

- Linda suggested putting big labels on cupboards and drawers. Frank had trouble remembering where things were, and she said it would be helpful for her, too, because she liked to have things neat and tidy.

- They thanked God for their friends, and were determined not to drift away from them. They would ask them to telephone at set times with a little news update.

- They wanted to celebrate their lives together. They would have some of their important photographs enlarged and framed to hang on the walls. And they would update their photograph album.

- They would try to take a half-hour walk each day. There's evidence that walking not only improves cardiovascular fitness but improves brain activity.[38] (Reuters reports a pilot study in the USA where agitation decreased and functioning improved in a group of elderly nursing home residents suffering from severe dementia, when they engaged in just thirty minutes of supervised exercise three times a week.)[39] After a time their friends became involved in the daily walk, calling over for Frank after work or at the weekend.

- Frank was not as sure-footed as he'd always been, so Linda decided to remove all the loose rugs wherever they were in the house. All their floors were covered with carpet or tiles.

- They agreed, too, that they'd have stronger lighting in some areas, particularly at the top of the stairs.

- They'd ask Matthew to fix handrails on the wall along the stairs.

Though Linda wondered how much Frank would remember,

agreeing the list together made them feel they were more in control, and it boosted Frank's sense of "agency" – that is, of being able to influence his world.

Making a risk assessment

As time passed Linda was to find a raft of other things that needed to be done – some that were quite unexpected. When they'd moved into the house years ago, they had found the ceramic tiles on the kitchen floor of such good quality that they had decided to leave them. Black and white and shiny, the tiles were arranged in smart, zigzag patterns. Linda noticed that Frank began to hesitate before entering the kitchen and would make his way around unsteadily, seemingly guiding himself by keeping a hand on countertops as he went. Then one day she saw him standing in the doorway, raising one leg higher than the other, as though he was preparing to climb steps. He didn't do this in any other room in the house, only the kitchen, and then particularly when he looked at the floor. Even though the floor had been unchanged all the years they'd lived in the house, she could see that it now appeared totally different to him. She'd already seen how he would seem to sense an extra, invisible step at the top and bottom of the stairs, and had been worried that he might fall one day. Looking at the kitchen tiles, she guessed that their pattern made them look like steps to him. So she had their son Matthew cover them over with a non-slip vinyl floor covering in a neutral colour, with no obvious pattern. He also stuck some reflective tape – the sort you can put on cyclists' and children's raincoats to make them visible in the dark – around the bottom and the top steps of the stairs. At the same time he made sure there were no trailing wires from electrical sockets. Linda bought a pair of new slippers with firm backs for Frank.

Knowing how much Frank loved gardening, Matthew made sure there were no slippery or uneven edges along the path, and he trimmed the bushes so none would catch Frank unawares. "It was virtually a risk assessment," Matthew said, "looking at everything differently – from the angle of what is the worst that could happen, and doing whatever you could to make sure it didn't."

Much of the unsteadiness of Alzheimer's patients is because the disease damages parts of the brain that affect vision, so their perceptions of colour, contrast and depth can be radically altered. I heard one caregiver suggest to another that she tried putting a black doormat in front of the door to dissuade her mother from going through it. Much good advice is available now from people who have been caregivers themselves. Joanne Koenig Coste looked after her husband when he had Alzheimer's, and after his death took a job in a nursing home. Now she is a nationally recognized expert and advocate in America for Alzheimer's patients and family care, and author of *Learning to Speak Alzheimer's*. Her tips include:

- leaving the light on in the bathroom at night;
- having a night-light in the bedroom;
- moving mirrors to get rid of confusing reflections and glares;
- running small Christmas-tree lights along the side of steps to give a clear outline of the steps;
- laying reflective tape along the carpet from where the person needs to get out of bed to the bathroom, so that at night he has that cue, and doesn't urinate in the wardrobe;
- making sure the toilet stands out in the bathroom, and

isn't lost in a sea of pale colours, by painting the walls a strong, contrasting colour.

Ms Coste painted her bathroom walls bright red, so that the white lavatory stood out. That might have helped Rhena Taylor, a missionary to Africa who came home to look after her father when he developed dementia. In her book, *Love in the Shadows*, she describes cleaning up after him when he mistook the edge of the bath for the lavatory. Toileting can be one of the most trying aspects of dementia care. Ms Coste trains nurses' aides, and tells them that if they see someone with dementia start to look around, they should get them to the bathroom quickly. "I need to go to the bathroom. Why don't you come with me?" is the best way to put it, she says.

Another helpful resource for practical ideas is a book by Sharon Fish Mooney, *Alzheimer's: Caring for Your Loved One, Caring for Yourself*.[40] Ms Mooney cared for her mother when she had dementia and is also a nurse and trainer. She gives dozens of tips, including many for the later stages of the illness. There are so many tips that it reads at times like a nursing manual, but that doesn't detract from its usefulness.

Just recently a husband enquired through Pilgrim Homes' website about finding an automatic light for the landing, with a narrow beam that would alert him if his wife went downstairs at night, instead of simply going to the bathroom and then back to bed. He didn't want a pressure pad that would alert a separate control centre but something quite simple that would let him know his wife might be on her way to the front door. His local Social Services weren't able to help with something as specific, but an electrician found what he needed at a local hardware store. Social Services are very helpful, and if they can't help directly they can usually point to an organization that can. In the UK, Age Concern is a great source of information.

New technologies that help

I used to wonder at the ambiguity of the big sign in Boots the Chemist that promised, "Aids for the handicapped". I haven't seen it lately, so someone may have pointed out that it seemed to be offering Acquired Immunodeficiency Syndrome to those who already had enough to cope with. Signs notwithstanding, the "aids" section of the store is getting ever larger, and there are also growing numbers of smaller shops and online suppliers offering the same kind of products. A national broadsheet newspaper recently devoted a double-page spread to gadgets and ingenious items, such as hands-free can openers, specially shaped cutlery and coloured crockery, three-legged walking-frames on wheels, chairs that lift incumbents up and tip them out, and motorized scooters. Most of them seemed to be for people who, while they are physically frail, are cognitively OK, but the need to care for people with dementia has prompted the development of a whole slew of other sorts of gadgets. They are like invisible eyes and ears, detecting, sending messages, watching and in some cases, reminding. They are called "assistive technologies".

Not far from me in South Wales is a "smart" house that has been fitted with a host of these devices. It is used for training carers, and nobody actually lives there. One of the friendliest is a small box that activates when the front door opens and plays a recorded message reminding the person to take the key with them and be sure to close the door behind them. The recording could be made by a relative – say, a son or daughter – so it would be personal and friendly. Many of us wouldn't mind at all being reminded to check that we have our keys and wallets when we leave the house, but sooner or later we would become accustomed to the voice and would no longer notice it. However, for people with dementia who can't store recent memories, the message will be fresh and effective every time. If the door is left open for too long, the device notifies a telecare control centre which then alerts a caregiver, who can go and check whether everything is in order. The "technology" alerts can be sent to different people – perhaps a support worker, or the manager of a sheltered housing scheme, or a caregiver in their own home. There are also sensors on both back and front doors which will tell the control centre if they are opened at odd times, such as very late at night or very early in the morning.

There are also movement sensors which note the absence of movement, which could mean the person has fallen; a door entry system so the occupant can see who is there before opening it; unobtrusive pressure pads that go under a mattress and raise an alarm if the person doesn't return to bed within a preset period; smoke, gas and water flooding alarms; detectors for temperature extremes; and a device to shut off the gas to the cooker, which must be very useful when someone decides to cook something at night when their caregiver is fast asleep. A thoughtful gadget is one that rouses the alarm without making a noise at night. A "pager" is connected to a vibrating pad placed under the pillow of a caregiver so that they can be awakened silently.

60 per cent of individuals with dementia will be involved in a "critical wandering incident" at least once during the progression of the illness, and many will wander more than once. Now there's help for this, too. The same global satellite positioning technology (GPS) used by the Sat Navs in our

cars is also being used in devices that can be worn, such as bracelets, buckles and shoes. Ann McRae of Anderson County, Tennessee, did everything she could to keep her husband, Pete, from wandering away from the house, but one day he was too fast for her. "I couldn't get him out of the middle of the road. The cars were just backed up," she told the local TV station. After her husband died in 2006 she launched a campaign for more help for dementia sufferers in Anderson County, and now each client of the programme she helped set up is given a bracelet with an embedded tracking device, which sends out a signal that can be detected within a one-mile radius. When someone goes missing they are usually found within thirty-five minutes, whereas, without the technology, the search can last as long as nine hours. In the UK, Fife Council's social work service, in partnership with the region's police, is weighing up the benefits of GPS technology for dementia patients.

Yet for all their sophistication and efficiency, the devices are only as good as the people responding to them. The manager who showed me over the "smart" house said, "All this depends heavily on the human team – on the people who handle the messages and do the backup. Another concern of mine is that, while all this technology is a help, will it lead to people living alone, without seeing a human being all day? Nothing can take the place of a human carer."

He was right – nothing takes the place of a human being. If technology were to reinforce isolation, it would be the antithesis of good treatment for people with dementia. Many charities have raised concerns about the growing number of older people living on their own, some not seeing another person from one day to the next. Imagine living with no human touches, no shared cups of tea and hugs, no mutual prayers or reminiscences, no one to reinforce your sense of identity and value. If life is all about the constant meeting of souls and relationships, a person living alone being monitored by technology would not be living but existing in a kind of mechanized twilight zone. Isolation could even have the effect of accelerating dementia, for feelings of isolation and loneliness produce the kind of negative biochemical environment that damages the brain.

Retired American psychologist, Richard Taylor, lives with dementia and writes and gives lectures. He has started more than fifty Internet chat rooms worldwide for Alzheimer's victims and their relatives. Speaking at a lecture in Sun City, Menifee, California, he said, "Alzheimer's patients and their caregivers need to realize the importance of interaction with other people in order to stimulate the brain." He is echoing leading psychiatrists, psychologists, neurologists and all the specialists in dementia care, though God said it first when he observed, "It is not good for the man to be alone" (Genesis 2:18). At a time when a prototype robot has been presented in Japan, designed to lift and help care for elderly patients, it's important to remember that humans were created to "work" with other humans.

As a help to memory for people in the early stages of dementia, Microsoft Research in Cambridge has developed a small, lightweight camera called a SenseCam. It takes pictures every thirty seconds, capturing everyday images to view on a computer later on. In its trial stages it sounds very promising. Although dementia prevents people laying down recent memories, the feelings associated with them remain. The SenseCam helps them remember the emotions attached to those events by replaying them, hopefully strengthening the cognitive memory at the same time. It's currently being trialled in different parts of the country.

Another practical aid to remembering is Reminiscence Therapy, especially with items that look further back to the past where the person's memories are still intact. It's recommended in the book we mentioned in Chapter 4, by Dr Habib Chaudhury, the Canadian expert in old age and dementia.

Neither Linda nor Frank had heard about Reminiscence Therapy, though it's coming to the fore rapidly now as more people look for ways of helping with dementia. It's something that we do when we sit down with our family photo albums or scrapbooks, or go through old storage chests. It's essentially the revisiting of past experiences that have positive emotional attachments, using as many senses as possible – sight, hearing, smelling and touching. So the therapy uses photographs, music and audio tapes, and things with "happy" and familiar scents such as apple pie, chocolate drinks, lavender, lemon balm, and even aftershaves like "Old Spice". All our care homes use Reminiscence Therapy, and I particularly like the corner in one of them with its shelves full of items from bygone years. (Did men really wear such stiff, hard collars that detached from their shirts and had to be stored in special boxes?) There are now Reminiscence picture books with themes such as "A day at the beach" and "Being at work", with big pictures and few words. Older people love them, and they're interesting for all ages.

A small warning might help if you're thinking of making a good Reminiscence "treasure chest". Janel, my daughter-in-law in California, carefully wrapped her children's first baby garments and tiny shoes and other precious mementoes in cotton wool and tissue paper, and sealed them in cardboard boxes in a rugged shed in the yard. When we opened the boxes one year, out leapt dozens of mice of all ages and sizes. Finding so much ideal nesting material, they'd transformed the boxes into virtual mouse cities with high-rise apartments, Gotham City style!

When I lived in Dubai it was a kaleidoscope of different nationalities and faces: Arabic (of course), Pakistani, Indian, Korean, Japanese, Filipino, Sri Lankan, British, French, American and Iranian – probably every nation except Israel was represented there. Faces all have the same features – two eyes, eyebrows, a nose and a mouth, yet each nationality had its own distinct stamp, and within those "brands" every face was unique. Only God could create a basic design that would result in billions of the same things, but each one recognizably different. We see the same thing in our lives. We all need to sleep, to eat, to breathe, to move, and we all carry out the same tasks in our day-to-day living. Yet each one of our lives is different. It's exactly the same in the lives of people with dementia. No two will be alike, but the practical steps and good care outlined in this book will be essential to each one.

POINTS TO PONDER

- Determine to keep a positive outlook after receiving the diagnosis.
- Make a "to do" list, for the long term as well as immediate steps.
- Make a risk assessment of the home. Ask Social Services to help, if necessary.
- Go through your home, making it as safe as possible. An occupational therapist could give invaluable advice.
- Ensure that the lighting is good, and make a clear outline of steps.
- Paint bathroom walls with colours that contrast with the

white lavatory.
- New technical gadgets can help. Ask Social Services about them.
- Ask about tracking devices for people who wander.
- Learn about Reminiscence Therapy.
- Remember – do all you can, then just "stand"! Leave the rest to the Lord.

Chapter 7

Tipping Points

That He would grant you, according to the riches
of His glory, to be strengthened with power through
His Spirit in the inner man.

Ephesians 3:16, NASB

"You were looking for the toilet, and here it is, in the bathroom," began Linda gently. "Here, let me help you with that zip." It was the week he'd begun forgetting why he'd made his way to the bathroom. He'd turn around and forget what he was doing, and then would leave and wet his trousers. When Linda explained that he wanted to use the toilet and tried to help him with his trousers, he'd get very angry and fight against her, pushing her away roughly. It took a long time to calm him down, and because of her arthritic hands she was suffering, too. Up till then, the only experience she'd had in this type of personal care was with her children when they were growing up. The training that caregivers are offered now by dementia charities and their local memory clinics had not even been thought of then. It was the first of many angry outbursts that left her confused, frightened and physically drained. She was grieved, too, because it was so unlike Frank and was another sign that she was losing him.

"Two of you start the journey together," said the wife of

a dementia sufferer, "but only one of you comes back." The marvel is that any come back at all. As well as the emotional and physical toll, they're also carrying a deepening sense of bereavement as their loved one is relentlessly eclipsed by the dementia. "The hardest part of this kind of illness is watching the person you love disappear from you – but you're still there," said a sad husband. A daughter who cared for her father said, "I got to see the loss in my life before he died and I was sorry to see that huge hole before it happened. I think now that my own pain was all about me. It was mourning."

Most of the time we tend to act reflexively; that is, we think and behave in ways that are intuitively individual to us. We see this in small and big things. For instance, when someone bumps into us we say, "Sorry," when it isn't our fault at all, because we instinctively want to avoid a confrontation.

I tested this with different people. "Tell me the first thing you would do if you were given a diagnosis of dementia," I asked. Their answers ranged from, "Spend all my money while I could still enjoy it", to "Put my affairs in order while I still knew what I was doing", to "Visit friends and relatives and tell them I love them", to "Make a will; get the best specialist I could." "Get all the literature and find out what help there is," said another person.

One of my close friends said, "Pray! I would pray! I would have everybody praying for me!" The friends whose first reaction was to pray have been missionaries for years, living by faith. At one stage in their ministry the husband was diagnosed with a rare form of mouth cancer that threatened not just his ability to speak in public (something he used to do a lot), but his life. Their prayer partners around the world took up arms in the Spirit, and he was one of the very small percentage who not only survived the treatment, but was relatively unaffected, and his public speaking is the same as ever.[41] The consultant was so pleased that he called his team into the room at the final visit, for their encouragement. "It's not often we have this result," he said. My friends' circumstances have taught them again and again where to look instinctively for all their resources.

Practical, down-to-earth Linda says, "When push comes to shove, you need to know Who to cling to." She knew that she needed to be "strengthened with power through His Spirit in the inner man" (Ephesians 3:16, NASB), and she chose a Scripture passage that would encourage her every time she read it. She wrote it on a large Post-it note and stuck it on the mirror in her bedroom. "For while we are in this tent, we groan and are burdened, because we do not wish to be unclothed but to be clothed with our heavenly dwelling, so that what is mortal may be swallowed up by life" (2 Corinthians 5:4). The anchor to this passage, Linda says, is the following verse: "Now it is God who has made us for this very purpose and has given us the Spirit as a deposit, guaranteeing what is to come." She says, "God knows we can't hang on to him, because we're too weak. So he gave us this kind of spiritual transponder, if you like."

It would be impossible to write a book like this without a reminder that, as Christians, we take a different view of life and death to people around us. We carry within us a sense of eternity and separateness, even though we are not fully conscious of it most of the time. We are pilgrims on our way Home. It is our magnetic north, and our inner person is being constantly drawn to it. Jesus didn't leave his followers to struggle through the rest of their lives depending on their own resources.

There's a story about a man about to be executed in 1854, who, hearing the priest reading from the Bible about heaven and hell as they walked to the gallows, said that he didn't believe it, but if he did, he would "get down on my hands and knees and crawl all over Great Britain, even if it were paved with pieces of broken glass, if I could just rescue one person from what you just told me."[42] If the story is true, the man whose perceptions were sharpened by the terror of what he was facing saw with piercing clarity the truth of heaven and hell, yet he chose not to believe it. Belief is not a mental assent to irrefutable facts: it is a choice that we make. The choice that Linda and Frank had made many years ago meant that when they found themselves ploughing through days of deep physical and emotional stress, like millions of other Christians before them, they knew that they were not alone.

Tough choices

The family still remains the cornerstone of care for older people. Most people prefer to look after their loved ones in their own homes, husbands and wives particularly. But fatigue – bone-aching, deep fatigue – becomes a debilitating, daily companion. A wife living not far from me was so exhausted at the end of the day that after getting her husband to bed, very often she would fall asleep for the night, fully clothed, on the living-room sofa. A daughter shared on a website that when she woke in the morning she had so little energy, she could hardly push off the bedsheets. A good night's sleep works wonders, but although caregivers desperately need it, they rarely get one. More often than not sleep patterns become disturbed in people with dementia, and they may wander through the house, waking caregivers and possibly endangering themselves.

Frank had been a "good sleeper" for most of his life, but this changed and he began getting up several times a night to go to the toilet. In the beginning Linda would awaken only slightly and Frank would return after a few minutes, but then he began to lose his way or forget what he was doing, and she would have to get out of bed and bring him back. She put locks on the internal doors so he would only be able to open the right door for the bathroom, but after a while, realizing that he was either getting lost or forgetting what he was supposed to be doing, she began to get up and go with him. She felt, at first, that she could learn to cope with less sleep, but found it made everything worse, even her arthritis. Poor sleep has been linked to depression, heart disease, strokes, lung disorders, traffic and industrial accidents, and divorce, yet is sometimes ignored as an important aspect of health.

An unusual programme in the United States provides caregivers with a night's good sleep, by giving dementia sufferers a safe environment for the night, away from home. They are collected from their homes and taken to a care complex where they spend from 7 p.m. to 7 a.m. painting, potting plants, dancing and talking – or, for those immobilized by their disease, relaxing amid music, massage and twinkling lights. They rest as they need, for a few minutes or a few hours, and return home the next morning fed, showered and, usually, "tuckered out".[43] Elderserve at Night is believed to be the only one of its kind in the country, if not the whole world, at the moment, though there obviously is a market for this service. The cost is $215 a night (about £132).

There's a greater awareness now of the need to support caregivers and, as we read earlier, one of the aims of the memory clinics is to do this with training programmes and social carers who can take the load temporarily. They also help arrange mini-breaks, from day centres to respite care. At a meeting of caregivers in Louisiana (which sounds typical of such meetings, wherever they are), people were asked what kind of information or help they needed in caring for a loved one with dementia. "A week's vacation," was the first response. The woman who called out the reply wasn't being flippant. "Most people wind up in a nursing home because their caregiver gets sicker," said the chairwoman of the group.

But experts say that it should be recognized from the outset that at some point, for the well-being of both caregivers and sufferers, the person with dementia will need to go into a nursing or residential care home. "This is not fatalism, but realism…" writes Oliver James; "it signals a wise investment in your loved one's future and the basis for continuing togetherness. At this stage it is in their best interests to be with their peers, so long as they are assisted by informed carers working on a rota system."[44] The key words here are "informed", which translates as "trained and fully briefed", and "rota system", which means that carers do not carry the burden of care incessantly, but hand over to others before going home for a break. It is totally unrealistic to expect one person to care on their own at the level of intensity needed for someone with dementia. That some people manage to do it for years is amazing, and says a lot for the power of love and the human spirit.

Physical crisis

There are said to be "tipping points" in any situation where one or two things become so great that the whole paradigm shifts. It isn't exactly the same as "the last straw", where one more added burden makes the whole situation collapse. A tipping point is more like a lever that moves slowly as weight is applied, but it changes outlook, attitude and subsequent behaviour. In dementia there are usually four tipping points: sleep deprivation, a breakdown in the health of the caregiver, an emotional watershed, and finally and perhaps most seriously, challenging behaviour.

When Matthew turned up at his parents' home one lunchtime, he found Linda slumped with her head on the kitchen table, utterly exhausted. Her arthritis was painful that morning, and she hadn't been able to help Frank get washed and dressed. He was still in his pyjamas in the living-room, watching television. Linda felt guilty that she couldn't help him: she felt constantly worn out and on top of everything else, her arthritis was getting worse by the day. Her doctor had tried changing the medication, but it hadn't made any difference. Now both she and Frank struggled with getting dressed, with buttons and fastenings. "I feel such a failure," she told Matthew, "but I don't know how I can go on like this." Matthew had never seen his normally resilient mother in such a low state.

He telephoned their local Social Services who, after a few visits and doctor's reports, arranged for a carer to come in each morning to help Frank get showered and dressed. While the carer was with Frank, Linda was able to go and do some shopping or other errands, and occasionally the carer would come with Frank and take him for a coffee while Linda shopped. The arrangement worked better than she could have hoped. Looking back, she thinks it helped Frank to live at home for a couple of years longer than he would have otherwise. "Frank was much more cooperative with the carer than he used to be with me!" she remembers. "It's probably because they are trained, and know what to do. They jolly people along and they don't have any nonsense." They've also benefited from a good night's sleep beforehand and are fresh when they come to work.

Matthew and Linda's experience in obtaining help was unusual, especially at that time. Most caregivers had to fight through layers of ignorance and indifference. It was, as many experts admitted, "a postcode lottery", with some local authorities educated and equipped to care, while others' cupboards were bare, both of understanding and resources.

Linda and Matthew are convinced that had Linda not had that help, her health would have eventually broken. For them it was a "tipping point" and they knew that eventually they would have to start thinking about a care home for Frank. Linda's pastor carefully pointed out that it's the responsibility of Christians to make the best provision for their loved ones, and the best provision for Frank would be in a care home with professional, trained carers, who took regular breaks and weren't sleep deprived. He reminded Linda that she needed to care for her own health, and that she would still "be there" for Frank when he was in the home, visiting and encouraging others to visit. He was also aware that after being caught up with Frank's needs for so long, life could seem very empty for Linda, left at home, and he made a mental note to keep an eye on her, when the time came.

For elderly people living on their own, the tipping point could come when they cannot be left safely to look after themselves. In the USA, Terry F. Townsend and his two sisters went to extraordinary lengths to keep their mother, who had Alzheimer's, safe in her home. They managed it for six years, setting in place systems of visitors and monitoring equipment that helped them keep an eye on her in every room in the house except the bathroom. For the visitors they organized a rota of volunteers to go in each day, including "a family member, friend, someone from church, or someone else that you trust, lives close by and can respond to any type of monitored emergency quickly", adding that they chose "only people you could trust with your life." Their tipping point was when they saw their mother fall "for the last time". They agreed that she needed to be "in a facility" where she would have help on hand the whole time.

Emotional crisis

The emotional watershed, or tipping point, depends very much on the people involved. For one wife, who had always been a bit of a "Mrs Bucket" (TV watchers will know it's pronounced "bouquet"), a lady very conscious of keeping up appearances and social standing, it was the way her husband began to dress, or rather not to dress, properly. From being a man who dressed very soberly as befitted his former job as a City executive, he became someone who insisted on wearing beach shorts with a suit jacket, a striped shirt and grey socks and shoes, and it became ever more bizarre. Dropping food down his front became the last straw. It didn't matter that he had lost the ability to understand his wife's objections; combined with everything else, it was too much for her and he went into a nursing home. It improved the well-being of them both. Relieved of the fear of appearing socially inferior and the daily, physical strain, she was much more relaxed and caring, and not feeling under constant opprobrium, he was much happier, too.

For others, it is when they become a stranger to their loved one. "I felt I had lost my own identity – I had lost myself, when my husband didn't recognize me," said one caregiver. She had coped well up till that point, and then was swamped with the feeling that there was no sense in struggling on. Within the role of a wife helping her husband she could cope, but when she became a stranger, the reason for being there seemed to vanish. With the help of professionals and her family she recovered, but she realized that her husband's needs had become too complex for her to handle.

It's always a shock when a husband doesn't recognize his wife, or a mother her own children. One night as Frank and Linda were getting into bed, he put out an arm as if to distance her and said, "Who are you? What are you doing?"

"Oh, come on, Frank, it's only me," she cajoled. "You know who I am – it's me, Linda!" She continued to talk quietly and he "calmed down" and got into bed. "It was all right, until the next time," she said, sadly.

It feels like rejection to the one who has been caring so patiently and lovingly. Sometimes the sufferer mistakes them for someone else. When she realized that her husband's aggression was not directed at her, but at the person he thought she was, one wife said she felt more able to accept his rejection. But the acceptance came when he was in a care home and she could reflect, calmly. "I don't react as often as I used to. I had to keep thinking, 'It's the illness that's talking'," she said. But she still has moments of overwhelming despair, and wonders if she should continue visiting him in his care home. Another wife that I know was amazed when her husband began accusing her of having affairs and cheating him out of money, until she realized that he thought she was his first wife, who had left him over thirty years ago.

Challenging behaviour

The main reason people come into care is when caregivers can't cope any longer with their challenging behaviour, according to our managers. "Challenging behaviour" covers a whole range of things, but can be summed up as actions that could pose a danger to dementia sufferers or to others, or behaviour that is antisocial within the context of living with others. Janet tells of a lady who used to forage in her neighbours' dustbins, tipping them up to spread out their contents. Although she wasn't endangering herself or anyone else, her neighbours and her daughter found it quite challenging!

It's generally understood now that "challenging behaviour" is the result of the person trying to express themselves in circumstances they are finding stressful or fearful. Although it is inexplicable and even alarming to others, it's often easier to understand when more is known about the person. No one understood why the gentle lady screamed non-stop when seated in the lounge where she could look through the window into the garden, until Dr Stokes discovered that on the window sill, where she could not miss seeing it, was a figurine of a cat – and she had a fierce terror of cats.[45]

It can also be the person reacting to unfeeling or insensitive behaviour on the part of others. A few months ago a television programme showed footage filmed secretly by a carer working for a domiciliary care agency – that is, where care is given in a person's home. The elderly gentleman was in the first stage of dementia. The carers let themselves into his home and behaved, from start to finish, as though he were an inanimate object. They changed his clothes, put his meal in front of him and moved him from one position to another without interacting with him as a person at all. He tried to speak to them but they ignored him. If he were to refuse to let them change his clothes, or threw his meal on the floor, this would be classed as "challenging behaviour". Yet, suffering with dementia, that would be the only way he could protest.

Dr Stokes tells the story of "Mrs O.", a lady whose behaviour, at times, made her seem like "the personification of madness".[46] Normally a very "kindly" lady, she would bite, scream, kick, punch, spit and in every way fight her carers, but it happened only when the dressings on her legs were changed or when she was being helped to the toilet. Finding out more about "Mrs O." revealed a history of sexual abuse as a child, and although she was now an adult, dementia had destroyed her ability to reason that the carers were trying to help her. Without the cognitive, rationalizing part of her brain, her past became her present. The ingenious answer was to move the treatment from the intimacy of a bedroom to a small room set up as a mini medical centre, with a screen and pieces of equipment that gave it a neutral, clinical setting. They also changed her toileting arrangement and, freed from the torment, she no longer attacked the care staff.

"Sometimes sufferers can resist when you are trying to help them, because they can't understand what you are trying to do," said an experienced dementia carer, "or they may misinterpret you. You may be speaking slowly and clearly, just trying to make yourself clear, and they may be thinking, 'This person is upset with me; they are mad at me.' Some things they pick up wrongly. It's because of the harm done by the disease process itself."

A message is a signal from one person to another, with the meaning in the message, and sometimes you have to pay very close attention to what someone with dementia is trying to say when they cannot articulate it. As you can see, there are many reasons why people with dementia become agitated or aggressive. It could be because they're feeling frightened, or humiliated. They're no longer able to cope with the everyday demands of life. We can all identify with that. When I see a child throwing a "hissy fit" in a busy store, I think that's what I'd like to do at frustrating times, too, only I know how to behave and I can control how I feel because the part of my brain that controls inhibition is not damaged. Or, like Frank, they could be feeling frustrated at not being able to do something they've done automatically for years, or they're not able to make themselves understood. Perhaps there's too much noise, too many people around, or they may be feeling disoriented.

Changing and bathing can be particularly stressful. Based on his observations of a care home in the USA, one author wrote that all people with dementia have problems with bathing, but Janet says that isn't the case at all – it's how you approach it. It's an intimate task that can rouse all sorts of feelings. Most people are not comfortable with being helped intimately or being seen unclothed, and good carers will be aware of this. A compassionate home manager made a special tent out of a bedsheet, with strategically placed slits, for one male resident so that he was never completely exposed when being bathed. Where possible, it's good advice to remove one article of clothing at a time and replace it with a clean one after washing. For showering or bathing, it's best to prepare the bathroom in advance, making sure the room is warm and welcoming, and gathering all supplies within easy reach. If they can be placed safely, aromatherapy candles with calming scents such as sandalwood and lavender may help. One of my reviewers, Fran, finds it very relaxing to soak in a deep bath surrounded by scented candles after a particularly stressful day with her "A" Level students. And talking through the process with the person is important, using familiar phrases.

Linda found during one period that getting Frank into the bathroom was the hardest part. He simply didn't seem to care if he was clean or not. She learnt not to ask but to simply state that it was time to wash, or tidy up, before a meal or a snack, because one of the family or friends were coming over. She found that it helped to put Frank's feet in a basin of warm water with a few drops of lemon balm first. He enjoyed it and it calmed him at the same time. "And in the shower I kept up a running commentary, so that he knew what I was doing all the time," she said. "I'd say, 'Right, Frank, now it's time to wash your hair. Aren't you blessed to have all this good hair! That's who Benji must get it from, this lovely hair...' I kept chatting merrily the whole time."

Wandering is also challenging, as it could endanger the sufferer, and causes great distress for their families. A patient with dementia in an American hospital was found frozen to death a few days later on the hospital roof, still in her nightclothes. Searchers had looked everywhere, but who would think to look for an elderly, confused lady on the rooftop? Wandering can be a very strong compulsion, and quite elderly folk will even climb through windows to go on their way. There are different thoughts as to why people wander, although rarely are they known, even to the person concerned. It could be that when the person wanders he is trying to find the familiar place where he once felt settled; or it could be simply that he is moving away from the place where he feels anxious, or perhaps he is looking for information, or thinks he is going back to work. Whatever the purpose at the beginning, it is soon forgotten, but the feeling of having a purpose remains, so he continues on his journey. Many of our memories are laid down with a sense of location, and it may be that it is the "location" part of the memory that is triggering a need to search.

If you read the acknowledgements at the start of this book, you'll know that Janet is a psychogeriatric nurse and a former home manager. The following advice is from a seminar she led at a conference we organized on dementia. First of all, she says, if someone with dementia starts to behave differently, check for a physical cause. Any physical discomfort or pain can mean a change in mood and behaviour. The person could be dehydrated (older people often have a lower awareness of thirst) or constipated, or could have a urine infection, which leads to confusion, restlessness and irritability.

If the person is being aggressive, try to think what the trigger could be – what's behind it? What is the person trying to say?

- Show that you understand that they are upset. You could say, "I can see that you're upset. Something's bothering you" – and make some guesses as to what it could be.
- The biggest challenge is often your own reaction. Try to stay calm, and neutral.
- Try distraction.
- If the person is being physically violent, make sure there's plenty of space between and around you. Don't close in on them, or try to restrain them – this tends to make things worse.
- If you're trying to get something done at that moment, ask yourself if you could do it later. Come back in five or ten minutes and gently try again.
- After the incident, try to behave normally, and be as reassuring as possible. Explain things calmly and in simple sentences, allowing the person more time to respond than they would have needed before the dementia.
- Find ways of avoiding or minimizing situations that trigger aggression. Check that they are all right, physically – are they drinking enough fluids, for example?
- Check, too, whether there is something they are objecting to. Does the person resent having his clothes selected for

him, for instance? Perhaps he would prefer a different sweater or pair of trousers.

- Try not to criticize or show any irritation that you may be feeling – and always praise any achievements, focusing on things the person can do, rather than what is no longer possible.
- Watch out for warning signs, such as anxiety, agitation or restlessness, and try to help the person feel calmer and reassured. Restlessness may be a sign of hunger, or thirst, constipation or pain, or of feeling ill. Other possibilities are boredom, anger or some other distress. Try to find the reason, and give reassurance. Try to distract them with an interesting activity, or by involving them in some form of exercise. Some people find a "rummage bag" helpful.
- If the person is not coping well generally, reduce any demands and make sure they have an unrushed and stress-free routine.
- Find activities to promote interest and well-being. Aromatherapy works well with many people. There is a good leaflet that you can download on the Alzheimer's Society website that describes aromatherapy.[47]
- Play music – especially Christian music that you know the person has always liked. If the person becomes agitated at a certain time of day, put some music on beforehand. The term "sun downing" is used in the United States to describe deterioration in the person's behaviour at this time of day, but it may not be anything to do with the change of light, but because of fatigue, or hunger, or needing to go to the toilet and not able to ask. In some care homes tea-time is when a new team of carers come in, and there can be a rush of activities. On the other hand, it could be because of lengthening shadows causing

uneasiness. Checking and eliminating triggers helps to give an answer.

* If there seems to be no pattern to the behaviour, and you are not coping, then seek professional advice.
* One of our carers recorded an incident on night duty. "Night duty again, winter's night, doing a round, cardigan on. Mrs C incontinent, so I fetch clean linen and get everything ready. 'You're not touching me, get out of my room!' she shouted, lashing out very aggressively and noisily. I go out, but know the job must be done. I wait five minutes and go back, removing my cardigan all ready for a confrontation and prepare myself for another onslaught. 'Hello, dear,' she says, 'come in – I'm pleased it's you. You'll help me, won't you? I like you – you love me, don't you, but don't let that one in the cardigan come near me, I can't stand her.'" It seems that, damaged by Alzheimer's, the person's altered perception meant that she didn't recognize the carer in her cardigan – but when she did recognize her, the most important thing was that she knew the carer loved her. Another proof that "love never fails".

POINTS TO PONDER

* Be aware that the continual grief that accompanies dementia may be harmful for the caregiver.
* Acknowledge that the sufferer, and the caregiver, will benefit from residential care at some point. Begin to prepare for it – see Chapter 8.
* If you live in the UK, remember that your doctor and Social Services can help you find help and support. But

often carers or social workers need to be asked, pointedly, "How can you help me in this instance?"

- Understand that there are "tipping points" in caregiving, and make an estimate of when yours will occur.
- There is a reason for the sufferer's "challenging behaviour". Try to prevent it occurring by anticipating and avoiding the triggers.

Chapter 8

Passport to Good Care

O Lord, You have searched me and known me.
You know my sitting down and my rising up; You
understand my thought afar off.

Psalm 139:1–2, NKJV

It was the time when the great financial institutions of America were beginning to crumble, just before the real effect of the economic meltdown began to take hold. It was like watching a great ocean tide being sucked out. People were left high and dry, mentally bracing themselves for when the tide came crashing back in with consequences they could barely imagine. I was sitting in my son's church in Southern California, the State that has been devastated more by the financial collapse than any other in America. Looking around his congregation that Sunday morning, the pastor of the Lamb's Fellowship church in Elsinore said, "We're going to go through some of the toughest times some of us have ever known. But we're going to go through them together. We are family – the family of God: from the oldest to the youngest. And families get to know each other. It's not enough to come here for the service or for the midweek meetings – we must get to know each other. Look around and ask who you could ask to come home with you this morning for lunch. Or some time during the week."

He reminded them that when the church was being formed a few years earlier, the whole congregation used to go for lunch together. "It was OK then because there were only about thirty-six of us and the restaurant could cope, but then we got to be sixty and then over a hundred and then more, so we had to stop," he added. "But if we're going to be able to care for one another, we need to know each other."

The importance of knowing a person was highlighted in an article in a national newspaper. Back in England, Dr Max Pemberton was called to a care home to examine an elderly man with dementia who was suspected of having a urinary infection. All he could see, he wrote, was "an elderly man with his mouth wide open, and dead, expressionless eyes." But the man's carer, Mark, insisted, "Did you see that? He curled his lip slightly. He always does that when there's something the matter... He's been doing it for a few days now." Dr Pemberton saw no change at all, but was struck that Mark knew his resident so well that he would notice tiny changes in his expression and from that could guess what was wrong. Mark was so insistent that something was, indeed, wrong, that the elderly chap was sent to hospital for tests. They showed that he had a urinary tract infection that had spread to his kidneys. It must have been painful, and it was thanks to Mark, and his concern, that he was not left to suffer, untreated.[48] Mark had taken the trouble to observe his resident very closely, and had learnt to read even the tiniest signals. I wondered how much information the home had been given about the gentleman when he first went in, and how much Mark had learnt by paying such close attention – whichever, Mark deserves a star!

Two thirds of dementia caregivers are said to be husbands or wives, partners who are close enough to know all there is to know about each other in terms of pre-dementia experience.

They've absorbed that knowledge effortlessly over the years and until dementia began to affect their relationship, could tell you as much about the other as they could about themselves.

When older people come into care because of physical frailty, they are usually able to tell you all about themselves. Their care plans are packed with all sorts of information, including their likes, dislikes, hobbies, past lives and so on, even their favourite colours. Occasionally, though, there will be someone who has lived or grown away from their family, or perhaps never had a close family. Or perhaps they have outlived all their family and friends. Frances Woodford became a published author at the age of ninety-four (*Dear Mr Bigelow: A Transatlantic Friendship*) and, being interviewed at the age of ninety-six on BBC Radio 4, she revealed a lively, interesting mind – but she was living a very solitary life. Did she see anything of her neighbours, she was asked. No, she didn't, only her own carer, and her neighbours also had their carers, she answered. Some people are solitary by nature, and are not known well by others. Once, at Christmas time, I did a quick survey of our homes and found that in each one there was at least one elderly resident who had no friends or relatives left alive. "If we didn't send them Christmas or birthday cards they wouldn't have any at all," a manager told me. To help make sure they are not forgotten, we remind their church fellowships a month in advance of their birthdays so they can send a greetings card. Pastors and others lead such busy lives, it would be easy to forget someone they hadn't seen for some time.

But when older people with dementia need residential care, the source of this information is their family, or their caregiver. This personal knowledge is vital for good care because it forms the basis of their treatment. An example is the lady with the cat phobia mentioned in an earlier chapter: if a relative had told care staff about it she would not have been seated in full view of the cat figurine and would have been spared hours of terror.

The best pharmaceuticals for dementia can only hold it back for a while and the real treatment – the "sandbags against the tide of unknowing"[49] – lies not in medication but in appropriate communication. "It's very different for people, say, with heart disease who can take a tablet every day. People with dementia need carers," delegates at a seminar were told by the Alzheimer's Australia education specialist. It's why the first thing a Scottish nurse decided to do when she was told she had dementia was to start writing a memory book. "It's basically a journal detailing my life history. I'm also compiling a picture book with photographs to illustrate my life through the ages. It's images and memories like this that can really help ensure the person inside the person with dementia is never forgotten," she said. Agnes has joined a Care Commission community group in Paisley, Scotland, and is hoping to encourage individuals with dementia in care homes to produce a memory book recording their history. She says that it has been shown to be a key factor in helping to treat dementia.[50]

The care is the treatment

In this pharmaceutical age we've come to expect either a pill or surgery for nearly every condition. It's why, I believe, we put up with the depersonalizing ethos of our hospitals. Although they are all about improving the lives of human beings, hospitals seem to be expert at ignoring the human being and highlighting the condition. They concentrate on what's wrong with you, rather than you, yourself; in fact, you leave all traces

138

of individuality at the door. I'm not sure if it's true, but there's a joke about staff referring to "the splenectomy in bed 4" or "the tonsillectomy in bed 6", even though your name is clearly on your records and above the bed. An acquaintance of mine, a psychologist and counsellor, spent a couple of weeks in hospital and asked his consultant, "Do you wonder what's going on with me, emotionally, psychologically?" "No, we don't have time for that," said the consultant. It's absolutely true – they don't. Signing me out after surgery last year, my consultant commented that it had taken longer than normal in recovery to wake me up. I said I was sorry I'd caused concern. "I wasn't worried," he said, "but we didn't have time to waste: we wanted to get on with the next patient." He was not being brusque; he was a considerate man who didn't rush patients at clinic. The financial and time pressures our hospitals operate under mean they have to be task oriented and, in general, it works. You go in with a condition and, hopefully, you come out without it, or at least, less of it.

It comes as something of a shock that the treatment of dementia is basically the personal care. With dementia the spotlight is on the person, not the condition, and the treatment is the care and attention they are given. It's why the person needs to be known as fully as possible – carers need to have all the relevant information. I'm repeating myself, but it's so important that this is understood. The Scottish nurse, Agnes, is aware of this, and is doing her best to supply it, ensuring that she will be seen for the person she really is, not the person she may seem to become as the illness progresses.

In these days of iPods and MP4 video players and the like, it would be marvellous if each elderly resident had a small screen, like a breastplate, that would activate when someone else approached, showing glimpses of them at different stages of their lives. Looking at 85-year-old Joy, in one of our homes, you would have no idea of the beautiful girl who gave up the comforts of civilized England for years of primitive life in the heart of Africa, or that Jill, now severely demented, was once a vibrant twenty-something nurse who didn't mind crossing rivers in a hollowed-out tree-trunk to reach people in rural Nepal, or being thrown into jail. Older people have such stories to tell. I interviewed a 103-year-old lady who remembered following the plough to help the reapers in rural Suffolk when she was a little girl. When she grew up the Lord told her to marry a man left to raise five children after his wife died. She obeyed and had a long, happy marriage, and the children loved her dearly.

We're a bit like Max Pemberton, in that all we generally see of older people is the outer shell; the "tent" that has become frayed and wrinkled. To be able to give the right treatment, we need to know the real people, and to do that we need all the information we can get. We can do what Agnes is doing, and produce a life journal. But we need, too, to produce an "executive summary" that will give carers distilled information about the person in a compact format. It's something that caregivers and family should begin soon after the diagnosis, or, if you are another "Agnes", as soon as you have been told you have dementia.

Who is this person?

The originator of SPECAL Care, Penny Garner, has developed a method for theming all this information to discover who this person was, long ago, and to set this alongside who they are now (with dementia), who they would have been anyway (without dementia), given their age and life experience, and what sort of life the person had always hoped to lead. This analysis provides a Care Profile which is carefully monitored using a simple caregiver tool called SPOT (SPECAL Observational Tracking). Then, as the dementia progresses, the information is distilled into a single sheet of paper, which she calls the SPECAL Passport. The first part of a SPECAL Passport presents a cameo of "the person". Reading the example in Oliver James' book,[51] you get a strong sense of the person it is describing: reflecting on it, you realize how much thought has gone into it. Take a mental step back for a moment and think about the key elements of yourself that could be captured in a single paragraph; something that could describe you. It isn't easy, unless you're someone whose work involves character observation, say a psychiatrist or psychologist, or author. How to capture the essence of a person on one piece of paper? Remember, this is not about the person you see now but about the real person, the way they used to be, and their main roles in life. It's about the person behind the wheel of the car, not about the faulty controls. It gives carers in a nutshell what they need to know in order to understand the person, and to really get alongside them, as Penny Garner did with Jack.

Try writing that first paragraph for someone who is close to you, now. I have written one as if for my husband, Tom. He died in 1995, but I'm sure he wouldn't mind. A large character with some distinct characteristics, he's among the host in heaven I'm looking forward to joining one day. For Tom I could write:

Tom is a retired engineer who spent many years overseas and is familiar with all sorts of pipe-work. His hobbies are cooking, photography, and New Orleans jazz. He is a man of few words who likes a quiet atmosphere and sitting listening to music and radio, especially traditional jazz. He has a keen wit. He only likes gentle television programmes, such as *The Last of the Summer Wine*. A sign that he is uncomfortable or becoming agitated is when he shrugs his right shoulder and sticks his chin out at the same time. He likes the New American Standard Bible and traditional hymns.

But before writing your own paragraph, watch the film, *The Notebook*, now available on DVD. More than anything I've seen, it shows how evoking a person's past can help make a link with the present. It wasn't made to educate people about dementia, and is a romantic love story; not the sort of film I'd normally watch. Our Director of Care and Housing recommended it to me, adding, "You'll need a box of tissues." But don't let that put you off.

The Notebook is the story of a couple who have been married to each other for most of their lives. They have children and grandchildren, and are devoted to one another. Then the wife develops dementia. After the diagnosis, knowing the outcome, she decides to write the story of their lives together, telling her husband that if he reads it to her, she will come back to him. We see her now in a nursing home, an old lady with dementia looking vacantly through her bedroom window. Her husband has a heart condition and has become a resident of the home to be near her, although it's clear that she doesn't know who he is at this stage. But each day he sits with her and reads the story she has written. The Notebook comes to life as their story unfolds, from the time they met until now. They have children now, and grandchildren, but she is unaware of them. Their daughter and her family come to visit and, sitting with him in the garden, she begs him to go back home and live with them. "We miss you, Dad, and Mom doesn't know you any more," she pleads. He tells her she doesn't understand. "That's my sweetheart in there," he answers, looking across the garden to the home. One day, as he reads another part of their story, there is a breakthrough and his wife "reappears" briefly. She remembers who they are, and their life together. It is only for a short while and dementia overwhelms her again, but it's long enough for him to tell her how much he loves her.

More than anything, *The Notebook* shows the power of love and of shared values and experiences. In case you are thinking this only happens in Hollywood, there are many instances of people "reappearing", or "rementing", as Professor Kitwood observed. It was, in his opinion, one of the strongest evidences that the current understanding of dementia was inadequate.[52] Dr Graham Stokes writes about a patient with deep dementia, who could hardly speak, yet who managed to convey to the team assessing his future care that, although he realized he couldn't go back home, he didn't want to return to the care home he'd been in previously. It's one of the most moving stories in Dr Stokes' book.[53] It illustrates, as do so many accounts, that the person has not disintegrated, but is overshadowed by the dementia. They are there but looking, as it were, "through a glass darkly".

It's described well by David Thomas, a psychiatrist with Parkinson's and Lewy Body Dementia, who runs a blog that has encouraged thousands of others, both caregivers and sufferers. As well as sharing his own experiences, David draws from a range of expert sources and presents the information in a way that non-medical people can understand. In September 2009 he wrote:

Something isn't right and I can't figure it out. I need to write this down. Haven't blogged for a while so maybe this will help. Haven't been able to blog. I don't know why. I don't know why on many things these days. Even typing is off. I need to start using spellchecker on everything now. I should even use it for email.

I was doing A-OK all summer long until sometime in August. I began having episodes of high blood pressure. It kept rising until I felt sickish. Fortunately I get an unusual type of headache only when the pressure goes up. That headache started and kept getting worse. I took my BP and it was high. It kept going up until it was almost 200 over 101. Couldn't reach family Dr or cardiologist. Ended up in ER for Rx and now am on a different pill with good results.

But things are different now. Am having a hard time trying to explain it to myself. Can't seem to describe it. If I can put it into words maybe it'll help me. I will try.

It's like looking out a glass window. Looks smeared. Never clear. Other times Vaseline-like marks are there. Can't seem to get a good look through it. Feeling trapped in my body or mind. Can't get it going. I think of things I should do but can't get up to do them. Immediately forget about them and then think about it the next day.

What happened yesterday? I think about the past a lot. Floods of memories. The present comes and goes. If I hear Pam and Chad talking then I don't hear the TV and vice versa. I look out at the trees and it seems like I'm looking through them with a blank stare. Feeling like I'm stuck in bubble-gum when I try to move. Fighting the shakes and tremors which come and go. They've been worse over the last couple of months. Especially the movements in my face. Muscles don't want to move right.

It's just now. In the moment. I see no future. I remember well how to do my crafts and how to use the computer. Guess they are well ingrained. Feeling some kind of apathy but don't think I'm depressed. Time perception gets altered. Confusion comes and goes erratically. Almost like I'm in a dream-like state. Like getting dreams mixed up with reality. Sometimes get sleep for no reason. Occasional feelings of feeling like I'm out of my body and feeling that things aren't real but I know they are. Can't seem to get motivated. I want to go out and trim off the dying flowers from summer, trim the shrubs, clean up outside… but it feels far away… way out there somewhere. So close in my mind but yet far away. I look out the window to all those flowers, veggies which I worked so hard on and now I see nothing. They are there but they are like faded memories. Seems like years ago when I worked with them.

I look at this and realize I'm babbling. Maybe hoping something will magically happen. Hoping to "snap out" of this fog or haze or… oh I don't know what to call it. Just that I know something is wrong. Am forgetting to eat. Chad made me a plate of food a little bit ago. I ate it little I guess. Pam asked me why I didn't eat much of it. I just now told her that it took me almost 1/2 hour to eat it. She told me I only took a bite. Oh, OK. She said it from a distance. Way over there somewhere. Guess I'll eat some more later. It doesn't feel important right now.

I need help but yet I can't explain how to ask for it. I keep thinking when I go to bed that I'll awaken feeling bright eyed and bushy tailed. I don't. I do remember to take my pills with coffee in the morning. I remember to check my email and browse the net. And I do some knitting. Ah, once in a while, I feel more alert and I'll occasionally write an email.

I have to go now. Am not finding much peace from writing this today. I'll read it tomorrow and it may help me more.

David's professional eye helps him note what is happening more clearly than most of us would be able to, and helps us feel what it is like to be trapped in the growing grip of dementia. He knows too, that one day he'll be walking around heaven with his loved ones, as right as rain. From time to time I leave a comment on his blog, http://knittingdoc.wordpress.com, and if I were leaving one today it would be: "See you there, David." Perhaps you could, too.

Getting to know you

All care and nursing homes are required to have a care plan for each resident. They start with a care and nursing needs assessment, which covers all the activities of daily living, and other documentation like risk assessments of many kinds. Then come Plans of Care which guide staff in how to care for the resident. Included in the care plan will be basic information such as how the person likes to be addressed; where he was born; his parents' occupations; the church he attended and for how long; his school and his feelings about his time there; his brothers and sisters; when he was married; his wife's name and children's names; the family pets; his favourite and most disliked foods and colours; and whether he likes baths or showers. This is information which must be recorded for any resident, regardless of dementia.

The SPECAL Passport lies at the very heart of the care plan for a person with dementia, rather like the core in an onion. The various sections which follow the introductory paragraph provide key information which has been developed through minute observation to help a carer handle a fluid situation at the point of action. The information has already been rigorously tested over time, and will provide crucial support on a repetitive basis for the rest of the person's life.

Pilgrim Homes' care plans are fairly extensive, and at the time of writing there's a Working Party talking with Penny Garner, looking at the SPECAL approach to see how it can benefit our "aged pilgrims". SPECAL is rooted in person-centred care, and some aspects are already in place, such as linking events in someone's past with the present, which we've done instinctively because of our shared experiences and values. Oliver James' *Contented Dementia* was published only in 2008, and although Penny Garner has poured thirty years' experience into the SPECAL method, it is still fairly new in terms of dissemination – as are the "counter-intuitive" methods described in the United States. With his background of caring for people with dementia, and his theological training and pastor's role, Roger believes that SPECAL is the way forward, and will be readily absorbed by different care providers.

A website giving advice about dementia care[54] noted that people with Alzheimer's who have "high levels of faith" show slower rates of mental decline, adding, "Whether spiritual

147

activities include prayer, religious services, or visits with someone who offers faith-based counsel, they have a therapeutic effect on many people with Alzheimer's disease. Spirituality and faith offer stress relief, hope, and reassurance." I've mentioned elsewhere how residents are calmed when Grace is said before meals, and at devotions. "What are the most calming, most helpful words for residents with dementia?" I asked our home managers. "Scripture verses," came the reply, "and the Psalms." Scripture verses have deep meaning for them. They've been loved and learnt, and have a deep hinterland for believers. Knowing the power of the words we use, Paul told the Ephesians to "Speak to one another with psalms, hymns and spiritual songs" (Ephesians 5:19). Christians in secular care homes must miss so much comfort and affirmation. With the care plan and the care Passport, the care home will usually have a pretty good picture of the individual's character, his likes and dislikes, and what is important to him spiritually. One of Tom's favourite old jazz classics was, "When the Saints Go Marching In", and he never listened to it without smiling. If he was a bit down one day and a carer played it, he would feel better immediately. With its upbeat tempo and picture of joyful entrance into heaven, it seemed to sum everything up. We'd lived away from Wales for years and when we were arranging a memorial service for Tom's family in Wales, the pastor of the old church that his grandfather had built asked me to tell him as much as I could about Tom. The pastor knew about traditional jazz and said he'd play something suitable at the beginning as people filed in, and to my surprise he chose "When the Saints…"

The thinking behind the Passport

The primary theme

The Bible says that believers are all priests – bringing things of God to the world and things of the world to God. Hebrews 5 describes the perfect high priest, saying, "he can deal gently with the ignorant and misguided, since he himself also is beset with weakness…" The main "weakness" of people with dementia is their inability to make sense of the present because of their short-term memory loss, so they will search their long-term memory for a comparable situation from the past. They may think they are in a departure lounge waiting for a plane, or in a war zone where they have to take shelter under a table. Others may think they are sitting in church, or getting ready to go to church. Or someone may think they are going to work in the kitchen. In Tom's case, he had spent many hours waiting in airport lounges and many months living in hotels, so being with others in a lounge would feel familiar to him.

The health theme

Nearly everyone has had a health problem at some time, large or small, when they needed other people's help. By invoking this old health problem, the individual can agree to accept help without loss of dignity or feeling they don't know what's going on.

"Remember what the surgeon said – you've got to look after yourself," would do it, for Tom. The motivation here isn't so much self-indulgence or hypochondria as respect for the medical opinion of experts. We might ignore advice from others, but rarely from our medical specialists.

Seeing beneath the question

"Pursue the things which make for peace and the building up of one another", says Romans 14:19 (NASB). If someone asks the same question repeatedly, it may be because they've been given a commonsense answer and the real reason for the question is still there. "Where's my husband?" may mean, "I feel defenceless without him", and instead of saying, "He's shopping, or he'll be here shortly", the best answer could be, "He's shopping, and he knows you're safe with us, here." Or, "When is my next appointment?" may really mean, "I'm anxious that I'll forget the time of my next appointment and I'll miss it." The best answer isn't simply to give the time of the appointment, but to add, "Don't worry, I'm coming with you and I'll make sure we get there on time." You'll need to find the right answer for more than one question, and often it's just trial and error. It helps if you know the person well. It is a joy when you "hit the right spot", because you know you've built the person's sense of well-being, and are giving the correct treatment for the condition. And don't forget, with a person with dementia you can repeat the right answer, again and again, and it will be as fresh to them as the first time you gave it.

Keeping the person engaged

Being lost for words, or feeling inadequate, makes people withdraw into themselves. Penny Garner recommends playing "verbal ping-pong", choosing three items from the various words, phrases or stories that might trigger a memory. The aim is to engage the person, so he will pick it up and lob it back to you. She suggests taking the part of the one with the less-than-perfect memory, from time to time throwing in the odd shot of, "Now, let me see, I'm not sure I remember what exactly happened that day…" Again, when you know someone very well, you have a lot of things to choose from, and of course, they would be things in the past, where memories are still intact. If it's of no interest, they will let the topic go past them, so you need to try another. Families have a lifetime of incidents they can share, and we, in the family of God, have a lifetime of shared practice. Whatever our denomination, most of us have read our Bibles. I can't think of any other group of people who have so much in common. We've shared similar services, hymns and events, usually over years and years. We can try a topic from that "old, old story" and see how it resonates. It takes time and patience, but it is worth it. The "ping-pong" and "spotting" and other SPECAL techniques can help us ignite the memories of Christians with dementia, so not only do they not get bored but can feel again the life and joy laid down with these memories.

Penny Garner says that having seen so many people enjoy their last years despite having dementia, she has lost all fear of it. "If I have to have a terminal condition, there's no doubt which one I would prefer, and it's dementia, as long as I have a SPECAL Passport and those around me know how to use it," she said. "If the dementia is properly managed, you can end up emotionally supported by the things in your life that you most enjoyed – and you don't get bored because the dementia has been used in a positive way in the design of care."[55]

When our elderly residents talk about their lives, they love telling you about the things that God has done for them. Some have lived through some very deep trials and tough times, but they'll only refer to them glancingly. It's the goodness of God that resonates. At 102 years of age, Ron told me, "When I look back on my life now, I can see God's hand in everything, from the start to the end." "God has been so kind to me,"

151

said 98-year-old Vera. With all these experiences, ping-pong and spotting the SPECAL way can be especially helpful for believers.

With heaven before us, it would be wonderful to say that if we develop dementia, properly managed, we would end up thinking all day about the things in our lives that we enjoyed most, because for most of us, they would be the things that God has done for us. We would be doing as Paul told the Philippians when he said, "Finally, brethren, whatever is true, whatever is honourable, whatever is right, whatever is pure, whatever is lovely, whatever is of good repute, if there is any excellence and if anything worthy of praise, dwell on these things" (Philippians 4:8, NASB).

POINTS TO PONDER

- Shortly after a diagnosis has been made, begin to think about putting together a SPECAL Care Profile for the person. You will then be able to prepare a SPECAL Passport for when the person moves to a care home.
- Practise drawing up, on a single piece of paper, the first paragraph of the SPECAL Passport for your person.
- Make a journal, a photo album and a memory box to remind other people of what is most important to the person.
- Remember that even in the deepest dementia, the person you know is still there. If you always recognize them, they will, in their own way, recognize you.
- Obtain a copy of the film, *The Notebook*.
- Read the book by Oliver James, *Contented Dementia*.
- A rich source of information is Dr David Thomas's blog,

at http://knittingdoc.wordpress.com

- The Psalms are a particular blessing for older people. They are among the Scripture verses that have been memorized, and they will resonate with good feelings from the past. Some will be favourites that they'll love to hear again and again. It is relaxing for you, too, as you don't have to be constantly looking for new themes. The old ones will be fresh each time!

- If you have questions about this chapter, go to our website, www.pilgrimhomes.org.uk and leave them on our Message Board. We will post answers.

Chapter 9

Minding the Care Funding Maze

"The silver is mine and the gold is mine," declares the Lord of hosts.

Haggai 2:8

"Mind how you go," an Irish friend of mine used to say as we parted. That's good advice when it comes to navigating the maze of care and funding systems for people with dementia. The dictionary says a maze is:

(a) An intricate, usually confusing network of interconnecting pathways, as in a garden; a labyrinth, and (b) A physical situation in which it is easy to get lost: a maze of bureaucratic divisions.[56]

It's a good description of the care sector today.

This is quite a long chapter and you may feel like skipping it. You may know all about the types of care available, and may not need to know about obtaining funding. However, there is something that everyone, including self-funders, needs to do while they are able, unless you are happy to see civil servants taking charge of your finances and charging you handsomely for the privilege.

"Secret court seizes £3.2bn from elderly" was the headline in a national newspaper, reporting on the activities of the little-known Court of Protection which was set up two years ago to act in the interests of people who have lost mental capacity. Around 23,000 cases a year, concerning people deemed unable to take their own decisions, including those with dementia, are heard by this private court. Where people have not legally appointed anyone to act on their behalf, their bank accounts are managed by civil servants from the Office of the Public Guardian (OPG). The OPG is currently controlling £3.2 billion of assets, according to the newspaper report. In the first eighteen months of its existence there were over 3,000 complaints from relatives, including allegations that officials failed to consult them, took huge fees from elderly people's accounts and have even searched their homes, unannounced and unaccompanied, searching for documents.

When a 76-year-old widow living in sheltered housing left her oven on and the fire brigade had to be called, without consulting her daughter, the local authority took over running her mother's bank account and charged her over £1,000 a year in fees. "All they were doing was ensuring her rent and utility bills were paid by direct debit," her daughter said.[57]

Other people's struggles with the system are shown on the internet support group, "Court of Protection Problems". In many cases relatives have been asked to complete a fifty-page form, giving disproportionate amounts of personal information about themselves, their family, their own finances and their relationship with the person they wish to help care for.

"There is something about [the State's] enormous, impersonal, loveless, bureaucratic nature that makes it needlessly suspicious, incapable of speed or efficiency, and inclined to bully," commented the newspaper's editorial column, adding, "A cold and grasping apparatus... treats applicants with callousness and suspicion, then demands heavy fees for its unwanted services."

The answer is for everyone to appoint someone to act as their Lasting Power of Attorney, should it be necessary. It doesn't look as though it's a difficult or costly thing to do, and forms can be downloaded from the internet, together with accompanying information. Ironically, one of the clearest websites is from the Office of the Public Guardian (http:// www.publicguardian.gov.uk/arrangements/how-to-lpa.htm). However, one of my reviewers tells me not to be deceived by the clarity of the website. She wrote:

> We registered our LPAs at the beginning of this year and did it ourselves. We found that solicitor's fees were going to cost us in the region of £500 each and when we learned that we could do it ourselves by downloading the forms from the net that is what we did – though actually we discovered that so much printing off and paper and ink would be involved that we got in touch with the Office of the Public Guardian (OPG) and they sent us all the forms, plus thick information booklets, and were really quite helpful. And all free of charge. They also answered queries over the phone – sometimes needing to go to a superior for clarification!

> But it still wasn't an easy thing to do. It was quite complicated and you had to have your wits about you. We both registered for the two LPAs – Property and Affairs and Personal Welfare. We each had three

attorneys, including each other, and then we also needed two witnesses, so there were several people to be in touch with and finding convenient times for them to fill in forms, witness signatures and so on, was not always easy.

The cost to register could be quite high. It was £150 per LPA per person (so £600 for a couple) when we did it, though this has been reduced now to £120. However, there are concessions according to income, which we obtained. These fees are subject to repayment if any part has to be done again as incorrect, or something is missed out, although when one small part in one of our forms had to be redone we didn't have to pay again.

The LPA is the former Enduring Power of Attorney and was changed to LPA about a year ago. It is alleged on some websites that it has thereby become much more bureaucratic and more expensive, which may be true.

So – time consuming, brain aching and potentially costly – but if completing the LPA keeps your finances out of the clutches of the Office of the Public Guardian, it would be worth it.

Entering the maze

Dementia seems to have taken our public health and social services by surprise. A high percentage of family doctors still say they don't have enough training to recognize it. Although it is a medical condition, it isn't treated like any other illness. So while there are well-trodden routes for cancer and any number of other diseases, the path for dementia treatment is still being beaten. The system is unfair to dementia sufferers, says the Nuffield Bioethics Council's report (October 2009):

> People with dementia experience a number of disadvantages in the current care system, especially in the way services are divided into "social" and "health" services. Many of their needs, for example for help with personal care, are classed as "social", despite the fact that the direct cause of their symptoms is progressive damage to the brain. Under the current system, this means that support services may only be made available when a crisis has already been reached because of the pressure on social services departments to prioritise those in greatest need.

> We argue… that dementia is a medical disorder and that the needs arising out of the disorder should therefore be met in the same way as those arising out of other serious illnesses such as cancer. It is not acceptable to make people with cancer wait until their support needs have reached a crisis before providing that support and nor should it be regarded as acceptable for people with dementia to wait in this way. The essential ethical point to be made is that the access of people with dementia to the services they need should not be determined by classifications of care. In allocating resources, and in determining standards of care, it should make no difference whether the intervention is classified as "health" or "social".[58]

Services weren't always sharply categorized as "health" or "social". The division was made some years ago, with the biggest difference between the two being the cost, both to the State and to the individual. Health care in the UK is free of charge, but social care is not, and if you need it you are expected to pay for it. Currently anyone with savings over £23,500 receives no State assistance towards the cost of social or personal care. But if you have less than that amount, Social Services will assess your means, and you will pay either a percentage of the cost, as Linda does, or none at all. The sort of care you receive depends on the outcome of your Social Services assessment, but often, as the Nuffield Bioethics Council noted, care is only made available when a crisis point has been reached.

This may change if a new National Care Service is implemented, as promised, in 2010. It is for around 350,000 people with the highest needs, who need help with every aspect of day-to-day living, from dressing to cooking – the sort who used to be cared for in a care (or previously nursing) home, though the National Care Service is to help them remain in their homes. To pay for it, up to £400 million a year will be taken from low-priority areas of the NHS budget, including marketing and communications. It could, perhaps, ease the weight of the £540 million that Laing & Buisson estimated local authorities would have to find annually to fund fair fees for care homes,[59] but I can't see NHS Trust Managers, who are probably not aware that they have "low-priority areas", being happy about it, so it seems to be a case of "watch this space". It may yet remain empty.

Different types of care

Years ago the term "care home" was unheard of and older people would be cared for in a "nursing home". These nursing homes were genteel, cosy places, a bit like comfortable hotels or guest houses. Sometimes people would plan to end their days in a nursing home, anticipating the comfort of being looked after and having all their needs met.

Then the government, that had been increasingly drawn into paying the fees of nursing home care for people who couldn't afford it, made the division discussed earlier, between medical and social care. Funding for residential and domiciliary (home) care comes out of the Social Services' budget and nursing care from the NHS budget.

Residential care is classed as "social" care, and the practice at the moment is for local authorities to take into account all the assets of the individual needing care, including their home. If necessary the home is sold, unless a spouse is still living in it, to pay toward the cost of care. In that way the local authority doesn't have to foot a hefty bill either for home care or residential care.

Respite care, where people stay in a care home for a limited period of time, so that caregivers can have a break, is growing. One of our managers, Phil, observes that funding for respite care seems to be relatively easy to obtain, as local authorities see it as an investment in the caregiver, enabling him or her to continue. Phil recommends that even where families have no contact with Social Services, they should make sure their elderly relative is registered with them, and in the system. He says families should do this even if funding is not required immediately, but anticipated at some future date.

Twenty per cent of all people over the age of sixty-five die in care homes and, according to care sector analysts Laing & Buisson, around 41 per cent of people pay for their own care – in effect, creating the market. But 59 per cent of residents – that is, most people – need State funding. This is a big headache for the government, which gave the impression a few years ago that it would rather care homes did not exist. Health Minister Stephen Ladyman said in Parliament that if you asked the average fifty-year-old whether he or she wanted to go into a care home, they would say "No". Well, of course they would. The average fifty- or sixty- or whatever-year-old doesn't want to go into hospital either, but they all want hospitals to be there when they need them. Ladyman was speaking as government funding was in the process of being switched from funding people in residential care to "domiciliary care" – that is, care in people's own homes in the community, and local authorities were given "switch-over" targets to reach.

Something like 6,000 care homes closed in the space of two years. As Laing & Buisson noted, if it were not for people with wealth enough to pay their own fees, and the existence of charities like ours, the residential care home sector would have been wiped out. Many of those who survived chose not to take residents funded by local authorities because they pay below the real cost of care. Leading charity Age Concern says the average shortfall is about £60 a week, and it will get worse unless more funding is released to local authorities from central government. Age Concern says that in many care homes, self-funders are cross-funding the cost of care for those with local authority funding, but that is not the case in charities such as ours, where the shortfall is made up from charitable giving. If it were not for our faithful supporters, hundreds of older people would have been deprived of our care.

At the same time that it slashed funding for residential care, the government threw into the mix an unprecedented slew of regulation. Meeting the cost of complying was a "double whammy" and was the last straw for many care homes already struggling with plummeting income. The regulations reach into every aspect of care operations, from risk assessments in the kitchen to the size of residents' rooms. One of the most absurd, to my mind, is that a carer on her way to work cannot buy a cream cake at the local bakery as a special treat for a resident who particularly likes them and has a birthday today. Cream cakes, along with any other dairy produce, have to be delivered in a temperature-controlled vehicle. Soft-boiled eggs are out of the question because they could contain harmful bacteria. When this regulation was introduced, some eight years ago, a group of residents wrote to the press saying they'd survived World War II, had eaten soft-boiled eggs all their lives and thought they were grown up enough to be able to choose how they wanted them now. Some regulations are necessary, of course, but very few of them, as far as I can see, touch the nub of the issue, which is the quality of care. Good care is something that comes from the heart, not the system.

But the care home sector has survived and Laing & Buisson estimate that the demand will increase as more and more people reach the age of eighty and over, the age when frailty and the prevalence of dementia increase.

All care and nursing homes in Great Britain have to be approved and registered by the government-appointed authority. This body has changed three times in the last few years, each change bringing another raft of regulations. It's difficult to see why these governing bodies need to change every few years, with all the expenditure that each change brings. The monies spent on changing the stationery, alone, would have funded a few hundred residents for a year or so. At the moment the regulatory body is the Care Quality Commission. Its website (http://www.cqc.org.uk/) gives a lot of information, though you will have to spend time stepping through various options. You can check homes' registrations and see copies of their inspection reports.

Residential care homes

Living in a care home means that your personal needs are met, twenty-four hours a day. Providing personal care, or social care, means helping someone do the things they would normally do for themselves, such as washing, dressing, showering, toileting, and so on; all the daily tasks of living that they can't do because of disability or the frailty of old age. Residents have their own bedrooms, increasingly with en suite facilities, but a care home will also have bathrooms with special equipment. There are communal rooms and gardens, and residents are encouraged to take part in a number of social activities. Those care homes that take dementia sufferers have to be specially registered, and staff are trained in dementia care. In fact, the training tends to be almost a continual process.

Clearly, there is a huge difference between being in a care home, in the company of others and with carers on hand all day and at night, and living in your own home where carers come in as scheduled for a few hours a day. There have been many press stories of older people who should have been in care homes being kept in their own homes with domiciliary care that hasn't met their needs, and stories about people wanting residential care but who can't obtain funding are common. An example is an elderly lady in a sheltered housing scheme who was clearly deteriorating and not able to look after herself (she was losing weight rapidly and falling), whose application for residential care was turned down by the local authority because, the social worker said, "We just don't have the budget. She'll have to wait until October." The scheme manager advised her family to keep pressing the local authority. One of our managers, a qualified nurse, "pressed" her local authority for over eighteen months for funding for her mother. A lady in her nineties, who was almost blind and totally deaf, was refused funding for residential care because she could get in and out of her bath, unaided. A former missionary with a painful degenerative disease of the spine couldn't obtain funding for some time.

Nursing care

Nursing homes' registration is distinct from that of care homes. The Royal College of Nurses says, "Nursing is the use of clinical judgment and the provision of care to enable people to promote, improve, maintain, or recover health or, when death is inevitable, to die peacefully."[60] It sounds the same as personal care, except for the inclusion of "clinical judgment". Nursing homes, and care homes with nursing wings, have to employ registered nurses. Two of our care homes have nursing wings, and some people there have come out of hospital under a programme of "continuing care". They wouldn't benefit by further hospital treatment, but still need some medical intervention and nursing care, which is funded by the NHS.

Domiciliary or home care

As mentioned earlier, domiciliary care was introduced to help support people in their own homes. Agencies providing domiciliary care have to be registered specifically under this category. When domiciliary care works well, it is a "godsend", but it doesn't cover many older people's needs completely. An obvious example of this is being able to get to the toilet at night. Most elderly people have trouble getting up from a prone position, or even out of a chair at times. In a care home help is available at night, but in individuals' own homes they have to wait for the carer to turn up at the scheduled time. For older people this means having to wear a pad at night. It is undignified and some observers say it "infantilizes" older people, but it's accepted as inevitable in the domiciliary care system. Again, many elderly people need help with getting out of bed and getting dressed in the morning, and if their carer is delayed they simply have to wait.

Another downside of domiciliary care is that, by keeping a person in their own home, they can become isolated. As a rule, older people have much smaller social circles than when they were younger, and many see no other person from one day to the next. Often the carer is the only person they see. Isolation is not only harmful for the well-being of older people (or indeed, people of any age), but studies have shown that it increases the risk of developing dementia.

Extra Care Housing

Extra Care Housing (ECH) is a fairly new concept in the UK, though there have been similar schemes, called "assisted living", in the United States for some time. The government says it has invested £80 million in local authorities and their housing partners between 2008 and 2010 to provide new Extra Care Housing units. Many local authorities have closed their care homes and built ECH schemes.

The similarity to assisted living is that people live in

their own homes, usually apartments (flats) in a purpose-built complex. Or it can be in a "village" scheme, with a mixture of houses, bungalows and apartment buildings that can be purchased or rented. There are facilities on site, such as a laundry, a restaurant and a hairdressing salon, but the main benefit is that when personal care is needed, it is given in the person's own home in the scheme. Usually a care team is on site at all times, so emergencies and unexpected needs are covered, and there is more flexibility in the timing. An ECH specialist said, "The carer can be helping Mrs Jones in No. 10 to get dressed, and Mrs Jones is able to do most things and likes to be as independent as possible. So the carer can help Mrs Jones get started, and then pop next door to Mr Smith, who needs help getting up out of bed." And older people can be helped at night, too. In each flat or bungalow there is a two-way voice connection to a Call Centre.

A good ECH scheme quickly becomes a community, where people can live and enjoy life and remain active. Our scheme in Yorkshire has grown into a lively Christian neighbourhood, and the residents there organize any number of social activities. They don't live in each other's pockets but the whole atmosphere says "community". In the main lounge on the ground floor (which doesn't have a television set) there is a large, unfinished jigsaw on a table, waiting to be completed by anyone with time to spare. There is a service each morning, and prayer and Bible studies at different times during the week, as well as a "Knit and Natter" group and art classes, among other things. People instinctively look out for each other, and when 89-year-old Annie brings back vegetables in the basket of her electric scooter from her allotment, she passes on what she doesn't need to her neighbours. Philip swiftly became the "technical" man, helping new residents install their computers and printers, and there's a lady who is known for her birthday cakes. Like all our schemes, Royd Court has its supporters, the "Friends of Royd Court", a group that includes residents as well as people from local churches, who meet regularly to discuss social and spiritual issues.

Information from the ECH schemes over the country is generally good, and interestingly, many report that the amount of care individuals need actually goes down when they move into a scheme like this from their own homes.

Sheltered housing and very sheltered housing

Sheltered housing used to mean individual units within a scheme where there was a warden keeping an eye on the occupants. But shortly after domiciliary care was introduced, wardens were axed, and now sheltered housing units either have a visiting warden or none at all. All the units, whether they are flats or bungalows, will have a connection to a Call Centre. Janet's mother lives in sheltered housing and she misses the warden very much, especially the morning call to see that she was all right. She misses the comfort of knowing that the warden is on site, should she need her, and getting dressed in time for the warden's call marked the beginning of her day, and helped give it structure. Many people in sheltered housing miss having someone call to see how they are.

Most of our schemes have sheltered housing in the same grounds as the residential care home. Some have bungalows, some apartments and a couple have houses. People living in sheltered housing join the residents in the care home for devotions and some activities, but if they need personal care it has to be provided by a domiciliary care agency, not the carers in the residential home.

The concept of the Good Samaritan does not exist in the sector's regulatory body. In one of our homes a few years ago the manager came to the rescue of a sheltered housing occupant who had been taken seriously ill at night. She wasn't able to contact her doctor and the paramedics at the nearest hospital were unavailable because they were already fully occupied. Because it was an emergency and the manager was a trained nurse, she was able to help her. Unbelievably, she was threatened by the local regulatory body with legal action and the loss of her residential care registration if she helped a sheltered housing occupant again, because she was registered not for domiciliary care, but for residential care. She, and the Society's Chief Executive, were threatened with criminal proceedings. Regulations and registration are very rigid.

Very sheltered housing is the same as sheltered housing, except people have their meals provided by the main care home and someone will call once a day to check that everything is in order. But if they need personal care, it's provided by a domiciliary care agency.

The assessment

The first step is to apply to your local Social Services, and they will arrange for you to have an assessment. There may be a wait, but if you need help to get out of bed in the mornings you should be noted as a priority. If somebody helps to care for you, they should be involved in the assessment, and Social Services shouldn't take their continuing care of you for granted. What they can do should be considered when your needs are being assessed. Carers need a break, and your carer can also ask to have a separate assessment of their own needs. The assessment is carried out by someone from Social Services, in your own home.

It helps if you make a list of what you want to tell them before the visit, and it may help to have a friend or relative with you, as they may remember things that you forget to mention. Put a notebook in a convenient place a couple of weeks before the visit, so you can note the things you need help with. Make your notes and what you tell the assessor as full as possible, because this will be the first time you have met and they will only know what you tell them about yourself. You should be given a written copy of your assessment; in fact you may be asked to sign it. If there's anything you don't agree with, or don't understand, add a little note of your own. Once your needs have been assessed, you will be given a care plan explaining what can be provided for you – and how. It may not meet all your needs, because there is a funding issue, as explained previously. Some local authorities can provide their own services; some will work with a voluntary organization or a domiciliary care agency; or they can offer you cash directly, to arrange and manage your own care. This is known as Direct Payments.

You should be given the name of the person who will be responsible for the care you receive, and they should check regularly that your services are all right and that your needs haven't changed. Whoever provides your services, Social Services is the body responsible for ensuring that they meet your needs. But, as the Age Concern leaflet points out, because there is only a limited amount of money available to them, they will often ration the amount of help they give. Local authorities set their own rules, often called "eligibility criteria", and in latter years these have been set tighter and tighter. There have been a few cases reported where a local authority has decided that an individual would be better served in a care home, and their home has been sold to pay the cost of their care.

If this care and funding maze has set your mind spinning, don't worry, you are not losing cognitive ability. If the British Memory Clinics work as promised, a key worker should be allocated to each family with dementia, and when it becomes clear that the sufferer is going to need care, of whatever sort, this key worker should be able to guide them through the funding application procedures. Without a key worker, your first call is your family doctor, who will then get in touch with Social Services. Social Services have lists of nursing and care homes in their area, and can give you information about them. You may have to ask specifically for a Christian care home – but it's something that you have the right to do. Care home managers are constantly dealing with Social Services, so they can give direction, too – at least, ours do.

As can be seen, the main constraints to care are the costs. The government has recently floated the notion of an insurance-style plan that would see all older people paying a premium of around £8,000 when they retire, whether they anticipate needing residential care or not. They would then be insured against the cost of care should they need it in the future. The Green Paper has met with disapproval from the Registered Nursing Home Association because it proposes to lay the cost only on working people who have retired, who have been paying taxes and social insurance all their lives, rather than spread the financial load across the whole of the working population. The proposal hasn't been passed through Parliament yet, so in the meantime, if you can pay, you do, and if you can't, you have to arrange funding through your local

Social Services Department. If the pattern of the last few years is repeated, then there will be continuing resistance to funding residential care, but if you've read this rather dry chapter, then you won't be surprised and will know how to push your way through. The social workers I've met have been caring and wanting to help, but the budgets they have to work within are the issue.

Because we're worth it

"UK can't afford its over-65s" was the headline to an article saying that the social care system is facing a time-bomb as life expectancy rises and the number of older people with Alzheimer's or Parkinson's increases. Other social commentators say that the problem is not having to provide for the over-65s, but the cost of other social programmes combined with the lost revenues of huge numbers of working-age people who are unemployed – nearly 3 million in July 2009, the highest figure since comparable records began.[61] Yet others point to the way finance is allocated to questionable programmes, and the millions of pounds lost in failed government and local authority projects, particularly computerized or information technology projects. "The money's there; it's how they choose to allocate it," said one pundit.

The issue of the cost of care for our elderly could have more significance than just rationing what's available. These costs are often reported sensationally in the media with an ageism bias that infers that the elderly are an unwanted burden. It was particularly disturbing to read readers' comments to an article about dementia care on a national newspaper website.

A number of people said they thought that euthanasia was the answer, because people with dementia have no quality of life. A few said that if they developed dementia they would look for ways to end their life. Together with fears about demographic time-bombs and an ever stronger movement towards euthanasia, these emerging views could have serious implications.

"Sentenced to death by the NHS"[62] was the headline of an article in the *Telegraph* after several leading experts signed a letter protesting about elderly patients being despatched before their time by being put on continuing sedation and having food and water withheld. (Google the headline and on the webpage you will see pages and pages of responses from grieving relatives and some from medical staff.) The Liverpool Care Pathway (LCP) was devised by a hospice in Liverpool in 2005 and has been adopted throughout our hospitals as a guideline to good, compassionate care for people who are dying. With its avoidance of aggressive, late-stage intervention and continuing sedation, it sounds like a peaceful way to die, and it seems that this was its intention. A good commentary on the pathway is given by the "Care not Killing" charity on its website. But there are deep concerns about the clinical judgments made as to when it should be applied.

The problem seems to be that in some cases people weren't dying until they were put on the pathway, but died as a result of it. Recently, a 76-year-old grandfather, Jack Jones, died within two weeks after being deprived of food and water on the LCP, only for a post-mortem examination to reveal that he had died of pneumonia, which could have been easily treated, not a recurrence of his cancer, as the diagnosis had been. Reports of his case brought a flurry of similar stories to the media. "We had my mother taken off the pathway," said one daughter, "and she had a further three, full years of life." It was bad clinical judgment that put Mr Jones on the LCP, but the fact that the pathway facilitated that judgment is worrying.

"Food and water are essential for life, so those who withhold food or water are, in effect, depriving a person of life," writes Dr Gillian Craig, Vice Chair of the Medical Ethics Alliance and former old age consultant. "Many people feel that this is morally wrong. Yet when politicians and economists want to limit the cost of health care matters of morality may carry little weight."[63] Gerald Warner, social commentator and writer, asked:

Could the most ardent fan of George Orwell have asked for a more classic, totalitarian euphemism than "the Liverpool Care Pathway"? That is the technical term employed by the NHS for a system of patient assessment that selects those deemed "close to death" for withdrawal of food and fluids or being placed on continuous sedation until they die. In 2007–08, 16.5 per cent of deaths in Britain resulted from continuous deep sedation – twice the rate of the Netherlands with its notorious culture of death and legalised euthanasia. The question has to be asked: is this euthanasia by the back door? Is the NHS getting rid of bed-blockers...[64]

Some worrying voices have been raised in the "life debate". Some say, in effect, that older people have had their day and resources shouldn't be wasted on them. And organizations such as the "Dignity in Death" lobby want assisted suicide made legal. Idiomatic is Baroness Warnock, medical ethics advisor to the government, who has said that "pensioners in mental decline are 'wasting people's lives'" and should be allowed to opt for euthanasia, even if they are not in pain. She insisted that there was "nothing wrong" with people being helped to die for the sake of their loved ones or society. In an interview with a church magazine, she went further by claiming that dementia sufferers should consider ending their lives through euthanasia because of the strain they put on their families and public services.[65]

It is an ungodly view, and is far from the truth. Ros Coward is a Professor of Journalism at Roehampton University, and has worked for many years as a freelance journalist contributing to several national newspapers and magazines. She also helps to care for her 86-year-old mother Sybil, who suffers from dementia. In an article in a national newspaper she wrote:

> If society begins to think of old people as needing to be tidied up and allowed to die when their useful lives are over, then we are preventing people experiencing looking after their loved ones with tenderness. As a society, we risk losing something of immeasurable value.
>
> Hospitals should not be concentrating on which people to save and which to let go, but on gentle care of the elderly. They should be looked after with love. This might sound idealistic – but shouldn't we be idealistic in this, if anything else?[66]

Jesus said that love is the kingpin to the whole gospel (Matthew 12:30, 33). More than being idealistic, looking after our elderly with love acknowledges that they – and we – have been made in the image of God. Standing on the platform of our conference in London on "The World, the Church and Older People", Dr James Grier, a distinguished professor of theology and an eminent writer, said, "When you look at me, what do you see? Do you see an ageing, balding man? You are looking at a man who, although he is ageing, is made in the image of God."

"We must stop the inhuman attitude which led to the death of Jack Jones becoming all pervasive – before it is too late," Ros Coward ends her article.[67s] If the proposed compulsory insurance scheme covers the cost of care, it could take the pressure off local authorities' budgets, and make obtaining funding a lot easier. It might make hospital stays safer for the elderly, too.

When members of the British Royal Family need medical care they get the best, whether it's direct treatment, or advice or convalescent care. Today's Royal Family will eventually pass into history but the family of God will live forever, and the Father God is mindful of how his precious ones are treated. Funding those who need care is clearly an issue for prayer.

POINTS TO PONDER

- The different levels of care available are domiciliary (home) care, sheltered housing, very sheltered housing, extra care housing (and some assisted living), residential care (in a care home), and nursing home care.
- Funding is available through local authorities' Social Services departments, but it is limited.
- Before funding is granted, a social worker will assess the individual's needs. These needs may not all be met, because of the funding available at the time.
- Make a note of all the things you need help with for a couple of weeks before the assessment.
- Having a friend or relative along for the assessment is a

good idea – they may remember things that the person forgets.

- Age Concern is a great source of advice and help. Your local Age Concern will be listed in the telephone directory.
- You may have to ask Social Services specifically for a Christian care home.
- Pray for wisdom for our government, and for people in places of influence, that they may make the right decisions concerning care of the elderly and those with dementia.

Chapter 10

Choosing a Care Home

My people will live in peaceful dwelling places, in secure homes, in undisturbed places of rest.

Isaiah 32:18

We're often asked at conferences, "What should you look for in a care home?" It's something that Matthew and Linda asked themselves, as Frank's condition deteriorated. They had reached the stage when Linda couldn't remember the time she last had an undisturbed night's sleep, and she was constantly tired. She was losing weight, and had constant muscle tension in her back, shoulders and neck. Her arthritis was not only more painful but was stiffening her hands and knees, and her fingers were swelling and changing shape. It was hard to turn doorknobs and taps, and buttoning her own clothes was a challenge, let alone Frank's. Matthew had fitted an electric can opener in the kitchen and had changed doorknobs and taps to levers where possible, and the carers had long since brought in a slatted seat that fitted across the bath to help Frank, but sometimes Linda felt so tired that she was glad to sit down on it herself. Every day brought a deepening depression and anxiety for her, and more difficulty concentrating.

Linda says she will always be grateful for the help they were given during those times. Their friends and people from church all pitched in. Social Services increased the number of carers' hours, and arranged for ready-cooked meals to be delivered and for Frank to go to a Day Unit twice a week. But, after a kind of holding pattern for five or six years, he began to go downhill quite rapidly, and Linda found it increasingly hard to care for him. She and Matthew and their doctor recognized that not only had she almost reached the point where she couldn't care for Frank, but her health was in danger of breaking down, and they asked Social Services for help in arranging for residential care for Frank. The worst thing for Linda was her growing feeling of guilt, and anger. "You feel that you ought to be able to cope," she said. "I feel that I'm letting Frank down by even thinking about a care home. I feel like I'm abandoning him. And I feel angry sometimes for no reason. Life wasn't supposed to be like this. It's not normal any more. I'm snapping over tiny things, and everything seems so out of control. I don't seem to have any patience left. Some days I wonder who's in the worse state, Frank or me."

Christian or secular care?

Choosing a care home is more than simply finding the best place for a loved one. It involves the needs of relatives and families, as well as the individual concerned. This was clear from a survey we conducted a couple of years ago to track changing trends. The survey forms were completed by members of over 100 churches, and among the findings were two contrasting views.

For older Christians, the most important thing was that care homes should be steeped in Christian values and practices. They wanted a daily routine, and an ethos that was a continuation of their familiar lives. They wanted to be free to continue to live as they always had. They had heaven in view, and distance here on earth was not a consideration. They were more focused on where they were going than where they were coming from.

But, for their children and other relatives, the home had to be within a reasonable travelling time. Typical was a daughter discussing options for her ageing parents. She and her husband had weighed up the possibility of a Christian home at some distance, or a secular home where she and her husband could call in every day on the way home from work. They decided that it would have to be the secular home, because visiting their parents in the Christian home would take the whole weekend, and they wouldn't be able to get there quickly if necessary. "Emotionally, it was not something we wanted," she said. I'm not sure if she asked her parents what they felt.

Whenever we have a dilemma, there's an answer in the Scriptures. Our Lord Jesus, as he was dying on the cross, gave his mother into the care of his disciple John. Jewish families had strong traditions of caring for their parents and Mary could have easily stayed with her other children in her own home. But Jesus knew the importance of Mary's spiritual life, and so, apparently, did Mary, for she obeyed, and went to live with John.

Residential care is something that's needed only towards the end of life as a rule, so families' emotional needs are clearly important. Perhaps the question is – whose needs are greatest at this stage, particularly if the person has dementia? If, as Christine Bryden so eloquently expressed, dementia is a journey to the core of the person, to their very essence, to their spirit, surely that calls for Christian wrap-around care and spiritual support? Even for older people without dementia, the Christian lifestyle is important, as we know from the enquiries we receive.

Typical is the solicitor who contacted us via our website, asking for information for one of his clients who was living in a well-run nursing home but "sorely missing Christian fellowship". The nearest home to his client is about 150 miles away, but his mind is made up. This kind of request isn't unusual. In each of our homes are people who have moved a long way just for the wrap-around Christian care and lifestyle.

But for older spouses, travelling any distance can be a challenge. Linda doesn't like driving: she's always been a nervous driver, and although her son Matthew says he'll take her to visit, Linda knows that he wouldn't find it easy to leave work early during the week, drive to her home and then take her any distance. Visits with Matthew would be restricted to the weekend. Her daughter, who lives nearer, hasn't been able to come to terms with her father's illness and hardly comes to visit any more. Frank and Linda's friends have said they'd be willing to take her to visit him, wherever he goes, and they'll be frequent callers themselves. But, even though he seems to be increasingly forgetting who she is, Linda is upset at the thought of Frank being cared for at a distance.

There isn't a Christian home in their region, but on her walks around the district with Frank, Linda had noticed a residential care home. About fifteen minutes' walk from their own home, it is one of the bigger, older houses in the district, set back off the street with a bit of a drive. Matthew queried whether or not his father would need to be in a specialized dementia unit, but the social worker had already explained that many care homes have staff who are trained in dementia care, and would be registered for people with dementia. She said she would find out more about the home Linda had spotted, but reminded them that the assessment had to be carried out first.

It was so much on Linda's mind that one morning, when

the carers were helping Frank and she had time to have her hair done, that she decided instead to walk around and make an appointment to talk to the home manager. Had the home been further away, she would have telephoned first, and she imagined she'd be seen by a secretary who would check the diary and make an appointment, but in the event the administrator who opened the door said the manager was available, and would she like to meet her now? The manager, Brenda, wasn't at all put out by Linda's unscheduled call. She invited her into her office, arranged for cups of tea, and they chatted for a few minutes before she showed Linda around. Linda remembers the enormous sense of relief when she realized how completely Brenda understood her situation. The home was a small one, with just twenty places, and nine of those were for people with dementia. It was one of a group of three homes, and Brenda and her husband owned all three. Her mother had died with dementia, and she told Linda that her aim in the homes was to make sure that everyone was cared for as though they were her mother. Linda recalls, "Everything in the home was so nicely done, with pretty cushions and flowers and comfortable chairs. It just felt like home."

If you'd asked Linda then what she thought she should look for in a home, she would have had very little idea, except that it should feel like home. She might have added that it should be "Clean and tidy, with cheerful carers and happy residents," and that would have summed it up more truly than she would have realized. *A good care home is a place where people are cherished.*

What do you need in a care home?

- *Is the care home registered for dementia care?* First, check that it is, and ask for a copy of the Service Users' Guide. (Our residents steadfastly ignore the "user" terminology – as far as they're concerned, they are *pilgrims*. They always were, and always will be.) Homes in the UK are required to give prospective residents a leaflet with this ugly title, telling you all you need to know about the home, including the residents' complaints procedure. It should include a copy of the contract. A good home will also have a friendly residents' information pack, with times of meals and other activities. As well as specialized training for carers, homes that care for people with dementia need secure buildings and gardens where people can meander, safely.

- *Visit beforehand.* You will visit the home beforehand, of course, perhaps more than once.

- *Check about the food*, and if special dietary needs can be met.

- *Are the staff happy to show you around?* A well-run home will be happy to show you around, and answer all your questions.

- *Ask how the staff are trained.* Who does the training, how is it given, and how often?

- *Check the equipment.* Look to see if the home has appropriate equipment, such as handrails, adjustable baths and armchairs.

- *Look at the gardens.* Do the home's gardens have comfortable seating places, and perhaps a gazebo or patio? Many people love gardens and being able to sit outside in the warmer weather. Dr Stokes tells of a resident, a very private individual, who found it difficult to be with others and found solitude and peace in the garden. "Kiss of the sun for pardon. Song of the birds for mirth. You're closer to God's heart in a garden than any place else on earth," wrote Dorothy Frances Gurney. Though off beam on all counts, it's a lovely line that captures the therapeutic effects of gardens, and most good care homes have them.

- *How does the home look?* Look around the home when you first enter. Is it a welcoming entrance, with information to hand, leaflets perhaps, and pictures? What about the atmosphere, and the smell? Is it pleasant and fresh? Is everything clean and well kept? But it doesn't have to be tidy; in fact it is probably better if it isn't tidy with everything neatly in place, any more than a normal home is at most times. It might have a "rummage box" or two in a prominent position, perhaps on a central table, where residents can come and help themselves, and it might have little crafts tables alongside the chairs, out of the way of walking-sticks and -frames but handy for the person in the chair. Rosie, one of our managers, describes the "rummage boxes" she has placed on a big table in the middle of the lounge. There are over two dozen boxes, full of interesting things to work with and to rummage through, with materials that are tactile, as well as colourful.

- *Look at the dining-room.* Are the tables arranged attractively? One of our residents told me, "When I stepped over the threshold I had a good feeling about the place. Then I saw the dining-room with the tables laid for tea, looking so pretty. I thought, if they take the trouble to make it look nice, then they care how people feel."

- *Remember the preferences of older people.* Don't make the mistake that one daughter made in assessing one of our homes for her mother. The daughter and her husband run a conference centre, and she is expert at seating people for all sorts of purposes, including seminars, focus groups, study groups and meals. She said to me, "The seating in the lounge is awful! Everyone sitting in chairs lined against the walls! They should be sitting in little groups of two or three." I explained that we had tried that, in more than one home, and all the residents objected. They like sitting around the room, with their chair backs against the walls. They like being in a position where they can see as much as possible, and watch what goes on. They don't have the energy for spirited tête-à-têtes most of the time. They leave their seats for other activities (and there are so many of these in the homes that I'm amazed they're not all exhausted!), but sitting in the main lounges against the walls is where they prefer to be. The chairs are rearranged for services and devotions, and they are comfortable with that because it's an arrangement they are very used to.

- *What do you think of the staff?* The most important aspect of any care home is its staff. Take time to notice how they interact with residents, and with each other. Are they friendly and welcoming, or are they "task oriented" and purposeful? Does the home operate a "person-centred care" or SPECAL approach, or something similar, or is it a stickler for routines and meeting objectives? Routines and objectives are important, but the only reason they exist is to serve people, not the other way around. It's actually easier to be task oriented than person centred. Tasks are more manageable and predictable – but not as interesting as people, and not as satisfying, either. It really is more blessed to give than to receive, especially when it's yourself that you're giving.

- *Look for care in the small things.* The Nuffield Bioethics Council recognizes this and says in its report: "The humanity with which assistance for everyday living is offered, especially help with eating and intimate care, is crucial in helping the person retain their self-esteem and dignity, as are the manner and tone in which a person is addressed; the care taken to ensure that they participate as much as they can, or wish in any decision about their day-to-day life; the trouble taken about appropriate and attractive food and environments; and access to meaningful activity."

- *Does the manager have time and empathy for you?* When you visit, does the manager have time for you, and give you her full attention? If you ask if pets are allowed, does she say, sadly, that they aren't, or is her response cool and efficient? One of our homes had a pet cat that the residents loved, despite his being plain to the point of ugly, though he also had a rather roguish air. When he died he was replaced by a pretty female kitten. You will talk to the manager and, if the home is of any size, to his or her deputy, who may be the care team leader. It's a sad fact that managers, who were attracted to the job in the first place because they were "people oriented", now have to spend a large part of their working day handling the paperwork and bureaucracy of increasing regulation. But the manager is your man, or woman, when it comes to weighing up the home, as it is their attitude that cascades through the ranks. I smile when I remember one of our home managers, now retired, who was so large-hearted that, like the Pied Piper, she seemed to sweep up elderly folk in her circle, and many of them ended up in her home.

- *Attitude towards visiting.* On the all-important issue of visiting, relatives should be free to visit at any time. We find that relatives are respectful of all residents, not just their own, and are friendly towards them; perhaps it's another "family thing".

Spiritual support

Old age has been described as the believer's last battle, when even the most robust, lifelong believer needs encouragement. It may not be as dire as in world-weary Solomon's Ecclesiastes, but age brings so much loss – loss of friends, of family and of people you trust, and even trust in your own judgment. Also, because they are not able to achieve as much as they used to, older people can feel that they have no purpose in life any more. Frailty triggers insecurity, which is a strong, pervasive emotion. It can affect even the sense of security in our salvation. Older people are often worried about their past sins and missed opportunities. A pastor told me of one of his fellowship, an elderly lady in hospital, who kept asking, "Will it be all right? Am I going to be all right?" Simply being surrounded by fellow believers is a comfort. Hearing the Psalms and Scripture verses that have been an important part of their lives is such a strong reassurance. Spiritual support is such an important factor for older Christians that we look at it a little more closely in the following chapter.

Recalling the calm that enveloped a patient with dementia every time a priest visited the ward, Dr Pemberton says that he clearly offered the patient something that no nurse or doctor ever could. "People exist in a social and cultural context that directly impacts on their health and how they understand and cope with illness – and for some people this includes a religious belief," he said. The National Secular Society had objected to a new scheme in which patients would have their religious and spiritual needs assessed when they were admitted, saying that it was an intrusion into the privacy of individuals coming into hospital for medical treatment. "I have to do far more intrusive things than asking if they are religious," Dr Pemberton said dryly. "For some people, when they are on a ward, feeling scared or lonely, people like Father Bruce can be a godsend."[68]

Residents in our homes are regularly visited by volunteers from local churches; they are cherished visitors to our homes, and pastors take special services, including on Sunday, for people who can't get to their own churches. The day begins with devotions; Grace is said before meals; supporters (again from local churches) call in regularly to befriend residents and make sure no one is lonely; and missionaries and other workers will come and give talks, usually with pictures, about their work. Groups of residents and sheltered housing occupants pray for various missionary works. There are probably other Christian homes like ours, where the threads of Christian life are woven through the warp and woof of daily life.

What is the best choice – a Christian care home, which may be some distance away, or the secular care home that is more convenient? There is no cut-and-dried answer. Much depends on the individuals and on the circumstances. I've mentioned already that in our homes are residents who have moved quite a distance to come in. Freddy's wife, Winifred, moved him by ambulance over 200 miles so that they could be in a Christian care home. The first morning of their stay they were able to go to the daily Bible study with the others, something Freddy hadn't been able to do for quite a few years. One man's family was worried because he was moving so far away from where he'd lived all his life, but he settled in so well that he became known as "the happy chap". But there are many more in secular homes, nearer their families.

It would make such a difference if people from local churches were more active in visiting those in care homes. It would be so helpful to have a kind of network where pastors would be told when someone had moved into a care home near them, in the way that chaplains in hospital are often informed when a church member is admitted. There is an organization in Eastbourne, called PARCHE, that encourages church members to visit people in care homes in the region. Workers from London City Mission regularly visit care homes and have some wonderful accounts of how God has encouraged older folk and brought many to faith.

I heard a pastor telling of the witness that his fellowship was, unintentionally, to the medical team he saw when he needed surgery. At least two of his "brothers" accompanied him every time he went to the hospital, and after surgery he had a steady stream of visitors from his fellowship to his bedside. Hospital staff commented on it. Going into a care home with dementia doesn't have the same sense of urgency as going into hospital for surgery, but it is a marvellous opportunity for our churches, especially when it is a secular care home. In the next chapter we'll look at the importance of these visits, with some guidelines.

POINTS TO PONDER

- Don't feel guilty if you have to consider a care home for your loved one. In the Bible there are accounts of how God "took and put" people into different homes at different stages of their lives. David lived at home, then in a palace, then in caves, and then in a palace. Joseph lived at home, then in Potiphar's house, then in jail, then in a royal palace. We're all destined for mansions in heaven! Remember that there will come a stage when your loved one is best served by teams of specially trained carers in a care or nursing home. Without the constant stress of caring, and being able to get a good night's sleep, you will feel stronger and clearer, and your relationship will be enriched.

- If you have been referred to a Memory Clinic by your doctor, you should be allocated a key worker to help you access all services. If you haven't been, ask the Memory Clinic for one. It's part of the government dementia strategy.

- Your local Social Services department will have a directory of nursing and care homes in your area.

- You can ask specifically for a Christian care home. You may have to be robust about this, as most Social Services departments have a "block booking" arrangement with secular care homes.

- If you need funding for residential care, Social Services will first need to carry out an assessment of the person needing care, and of the caregiver.

- Before you visit a prospective care home, make a list of the points mentioned here, and take it with you.

- Ask the home for a copy of its "Service User Guide".

- People with dementia are not considered for nursing care, only personal or social care.

- You can download a copy of the Nuffield Bioethics Council guide on http://www.nuffieldbioethics.org/go/ourwork/dementia/publication_530.html

- As we grow older, we realize how deeply our identity is grounded in Christ. Shared values and beliefs contribute hugely to a person's well-being. If you can't find a Christian care home near you, try to arrange for regular visits from members of your church. Our booklet *How to help those with dementia* gives practical guidelines, and can be downloaded through our website.

Chapter 11

Visiting and Spiritual Support

The King will reply, "I tell you the truth, whatever you did for one of the least of these brothers of mine, you did for me."

MATTHEW 25:40

"I thought, having covered wars, I'd be able to cope," said TV news presenter John Suchet after taking his wife Bonnie to live in a care home. But the trauma of wars did not compare to the grief he felt at having to leave her, even though it was a lovely care home that he knows he is privileged to be able to afford. "Given my advantages, it's still destroyed me, absolutely torn me apart," he told the interviewer.[69] When Bonnie was living at home she was cared for by an Admiral Nurse, trained specifically in caring for people with dementia. The nurse explained to John that he was in mourning for the Bonnie he had lost, telling him, "You are suffering, in a way, more than she is."

"Arranging for a close family member to go into care is just about the worst thing that they have ever had to do", Revd Malcolm Goldsmith writes, quoting the American writer (Renee Shield, 1997) who said that the nursing home "symbolically embodies the dangerous transition from adulthood to death."[70] I'm not sure if Christians would see that transition as "dangerous"; we see physical death as a gateway to something far better. It's that "internal transponder" mentioned earlier at work in us; the "Christ in you, the hope of glory" that Colossians 1:27 describes. If we really believe all that Jesus said, we should not have the same view of death as unbelievers.

Nevertheless, taking someone to live in a care home is a major milestone on the long "goodbye" road of dementia. Afterwards, finding themselves alone for the first time in years, caregivers struggle with deep emotions, the strongest of which is a sense of failure, followed by guilt. Nearly everyone thinks they should have been able to manage, and they shouldn't feel angry or guilty. But nearly every caregiver does, especially we Christians, with our unattainably high standards. Unattainably high? Of course they are. They are there to draw us up higher. As Paul wrote to the Christians at Philippi: "Brethren, I count not myself to have apprehended: but this one thing I do, forgetting those things which are behind, and reaching forth unto those things which are before, I press toward the mark for the prize of the high calling of God in Christ Jesus." (Philippians 3:13–14, KJV). We will never be perfect this side of Glory. Physically, too, the recovery is not always as quick as might be expected; the toll on many caregivers is very high.

Linda and Frank are one of the thousands of couples who have shared experiences similar to those of John and Bonnie Suchet, except they are amongst the 59 per cent of people who can't afford the cost of care. Frank's care was funded by their local authority, after an assessment by Social Services, which had been influenced as much by Linda's physical deterioration as by Frank's. Frank had become very unsettled, and even his favourite films failed to hold his attention as they once had. He took to pacing around the house and garden during the day as well as at night, trying to open the front door and reacting with anger when he found it locked. On two occasions he'd dialled the emergency police number, and police officers had turned up at the door. He had been falling down more and more and Linda had been finding it increasingly difficult to help get him up. There had been a frightening incident one day when he fell and knocked her down too, landing on top of her and pinning them both to the ground. She still can't remember how she managed to get them up. When the carer arrived later that day she was still shaking and in pain, and Frank had a badly twisted ankle. A couple of times she'd had to call out the Paramedics team from her local Accident & Emergency Department. Linda felt her depression was almost as deep as Frank's.

Social Services also agreed that the home nearby was suitable, and "by God's grace", says Linda, the home had a vacancy. She and Matthew took Frank in just before lunch one morning and helped him to settle in. They put some of his special mementoes in his room, including his big model of the Peterbild truck from America, some family photographs – especially a big one of Benji – and his favourite bedside chair. "He seemed to be very much in his own world that day," Linda remembers. "Over lunch Matthew and I were chatting and trying to draw him out of himself, but he just didn't seem to be interested in anything."

Because the home is within walking distance, Linda is able to visit Frank every day, and Matthew drives up as often as he can – usually at the weekend. Their friends visit a couple of times a week, and their Pastor, Harry, calls in at least once a week. The quality of their visits varies, depending on how Frank is at the time, but Linda has explained that even if Frank doesn't seem to be responding to them, it's good for him to have company.

The psychiatrist with dementia, David Thomas, said the same thing. He'd written in his blog about one of his worse days, when he seemed to be weighted with apathy and inertia, and looking at life through a smeary glass (see Chapter 8). A reader asked how he would like people to react to him at times like that:

> Do you want people to talk to you? Would you like them to take you for a walk, or to try and bring you out of the fog? Or would you prefer to be left alone? Or do you want people to just be around, but not saying anything? Of course everyone is different, but I think understanding your views would be helpful.

In a reply that throws light in a way that only someone with dementia could do, David replied:

> I think that I prefer people around me but not feeling as though they have to speak and interact with me. It's a pressure I don't want to put upon them. If people try to talk to me, then it gets very frustrating because things don't always make sense or I feel I have to respond at a time that I'm not clearheaded or that I can find the right words.

> Definitely not try to make me walk or do something at that moment. Being left alone is OK most of the time. Sometimes I feel frightened for no reason and go shut and lock the doors and close the blinds. Not often, significant when I do.

I would imagine that this answer would vary from person to person with dementia based upon their personality, etc.

Definitely don't try to snap me out of it. If I could snap out of it, I would do it and then there wouldn't be a problem. Kind of like trying to get someone to stop crying whenever a close loved one dies. Trying to get them to snap out of it and to begin laughing joyously is not very kind in my thinking. We all have to go through various emotions and states naturally.

I'm not sure if any of this makes any sense. If it doesn't, let me know and I try to explain it differently.

Overall, I think having people around but not necessarily interacting works the best for me. Following my lead would be the clue. If I wanted/tried to interact, then follow along. Otherwise, just be in the moment with me.

"Having people around but not necessarily interacting" sounds very comfortable. I remember seeing a lady in hospital, comfortably propped up in bed while her children visited. They sat around her bed, talking with each other and looking to her from time to time to see if she wanted to interact. Mostly she didn't, so they continued visiting with each other, allowing her to relax and enjoy their company without having to make any effort herself. Conversation demands interaction, and that takes energy, whereas just sitting and keeping someone company is undemanding, and peaceful. One of my favourite songs could have been written for times like these. It's one of the most enduring songs of all time, by Billy Joel, and begins,

"I wouldn't leave you in times of trouble…" and goes on to say that as well as the good times, he'll take the bad times, adding, "I'll take you just the way you are." The song goes on to say that he doesn't need clever conversation, either. In fact, keeping people company can be very restful with no conversation at all.

Two or three people could visit someone with dementia in this way. They could read the Bible and pray, and discuss spiritual things. "Don't abandon me at any stage, for the Holy Spirit connects us," pleaded dementia sufferer Christine Bryden at a conference. "I need you to minister to me, to sing with me, pray with me… You play a vital role in relating to the soul within me, connecting at this eternal level. Sing alongside me, touch me, pray with me, reassure me of your presence, and through you, of Christ's presence." They could leave a space for the person to respond, but as David said, they could take the person's lead, and it would not be at all stressful for anyone.

Learning from children

Have you ever noticed how children can be with each other at times without making conversation? They haven't built the list of "oughts" and "shoulds" that adults carry around with them, so they are free to be themselves. We could learn a lot from them when it comes to visiting older people.

Five-year-old Patrick Wader loves visiting the nursing home where his father works in Davenport, Iowa. He helps plan events for the Alzheimer's patients and they love him. Asked why he likes spending time with people who are old enough to be his great grandparents and who sometimes can't remember the names of their own children, he answered, "I like them. I help 'em make crafts and colour with 'em. They like kids. They have fun with kids." A home executive said he had heard that Patrick had managed to coax some residents out of their rooms, even though they had refused to leave them in the past. He said, "He's happy to be around people, and I think that rubs off on the people in the dementia unit. He really enjoys them, and they enjoy him. That's what's important."[71]

"When young boys visit a nursing home, miracles occur", was the headline of a story of a teacher taking her class of ten boys to visit a nursing home. "Ten boys, and all friends!" she stressed. (Only teachers and mothers of boys really understand the meaning of that!) They were to sing a song to the residents, and had to be dissuaded from rehearsing "Staying Alive", because that's what they thought the old folks would want. So they rehearsed something more suitable instead. Off they went, pushing and shoving as boys do, but they lapsed into awed silence once inside, because they'd never seen so many old folk in wheelchairs, or napping, or sitting together in one place. As the boys started to sing, the teacher wrote, "Eyes began shining, bodies became more alert and shifted in chairs to get a better look, smiles appeared from every corner of the room." After the song the boys were introduced to each resident, with snippets of information about each one. This lady once sang for the Metropolitan Opera; this man was a writer; this lady had raised eight children. "These people weren't always old," the manager told the boys, who listened carefully. "They were someone's baby, then they were like you, and then they grew up! They had jobs, had families and now they are here: they're real people who have had a very important life." Small hands reached out, and older voices responded, telling a little about themselves – how many books had been written and other things they'd done. "Grey heads and heads the vibrant colours of healthy youth bent toward each other to talk and then to carefully listen, and wrinkled hands held small strong hands for a short time before we moved on…"[72]

Some of our homes are fairly near local schools, and school children come to visit from time to time. At Christmas time they come and sing Christmas carols, and at Harvest Thanksgiving there are pictures of smiling children standing happily next to tables of produce they've brought. A Second World War anniversary was an opportunity for children to visit another home and record interviews with residents about their wartime memories. The children found their stories fascinating, and the residents loved being able to tell them.

There's a unique rapport between older people and young children; something I believe God has built in so that our elders can pass on to these little ones stories of his goodness and accounts of his faithfulness. Psalm 78 says:

For He established a testimony in Jacob and appointed a law in Israel, Which he commanded our fathers that they should teach them to their children, that the generation to come might know, even the children yet to be born, that they may arise and tell them to their children, That they should put their confidence in God and not forget the works of God. (NASB)

"Blood is thicker than water," is the old saying about families. It's true, too; but the Calvary blood that binds the family of God is stronger and deeper than we realize. There is a strong bond in the family of God, whatever our denomination. It's a "family thing" for our Home Visitors, who do their best to ensure that none of our residents are lonely. Our Home Visitors are people from local churches who join our homes' support groups to befriend their residents. They visit them in hospital, too, if necessary. I have a picture of a Home Visitor and a resident that really does say more than a thousand words.

In one of our homes, two ladies were sitting close together deep in conversation, their eyes locked. One was frail and elderly, wearing a pretty print dress and the other, a generation or two younger, wore a winter hat and an incredibly kind expression. Supporting the older lady's hand as though it were as delicate as a feather, the visitor smiled as she talked, and the resident's face glowed with contentment. I wanted to capture the moment to share with others, so I turned into the lounge and asked if they minded if I took a photograph of them while they talked. "Not at all," said the visitor. "Is it all right with you?" I asked the resident. Her answer was so soft and indistinct that I had to bend to hear, then I realized that she was suffering from dementia. But even though her words were jumbled and indistinguishable, she was trying to give me an answer, so I leaned in even closer and cupped my hand round my ear. "Dear me," I said, "I'm not hearing very well today. But I think you're saying that you don't mind if I take a photograph of you both." She relaxed and her face lit up, so we could see, the visitor and I, that we'd made a good connection and that she was happy to be photographed.

As I unpacked my camera the visitor turned to her and, making the same, sure connection with her eyes, took up where she'd left off. "Trust in the Lord with all your heart," she continued, with the same lovely smile, "and lean not to your own understanding. That's what the Scripture says..." And so she went on. The older lady sat contentedly, simply soaking up the words, and you could sense her spirit expanding in the moment. I didn't get the picture I wanted because my camera and I were something of a distraction, but it's a scene that plays in our homes over and over again as visitors and staff encourage elderly residents with the beloved Scripture verses that have been so much a part of their lives.

This particular visitor had experience of dementia, as two of her relatives had died with it, but many people feel at a loss when visiting, particularly when the person doesn't seem to recognize them, or will forget their visit the moment they leave. It may not make sense to you, but it doesn't matter whether they remember your visit or not; but they will remember the feeling that your visit brought them. It doesn't matter if they don't recognize you, either; but by being there, by being in relationship with them and honouring the "Thou", you are affirming their worth. You are bringing Christ's presence with you.

Matthew 25:40 is often quoted in connection with good works, including evangelism, but if you read it you'll see Jesus is talking about his brethren – that is, those who belong to the family of God. I'm probably repeating myself again but, if the "Christ in us" is in the body of a person whose brain is damaged by dementia, who's forgotten how to eat and talk – people who might feel they fill the description of "the least of my brethren" – isn't Jesus going to know those who "did it for Me?"

Don't talk of love, show me!

A chapter in Malcolm Goldsmith's book on people with dementia and the local church is entitled *Don't talk of love, show me!* Perhaps there's never been a better time for people who tell others of the love of God to show it to family members struggling with dementia – both sufferers and caregivers. One of the most pointed questions at one of our dementia conferences came from a church leader who asked, "In the light of the rising numbers of people with dementia, how can we in the Christian church be prepared to help?" In the coming months we plan to put together a Dementia Information Pack for churches in response to many questions like this. In the meantime, the following are examples of the advice we are giving.

The first piece of advice is: *Just do it!* Remember that we are God's children, Christ's purchased possession. Never assume that frailty and confusion exclude the work of the Holy Spirit (Hebrews 13:5). Don't stay away from people with dementia when they've been a part of your fellowship or your circle. They are still in your "bundle of the living" (1 Samuel 25:29), and now this has happened to them, they need you more than ever. Whether the person is still living at home or is in a care home, there are some practical things you can do to make your visits a blessing.

Before your visit

Pray before you go. Find out as much as possible about the person with dementia. If you used to know them well but have dropped out of touch, their caregiver can bring you up to date. Some phrases will be especially meaningful and comforting to them, and can act as triggers for good or for bad! And ask how they like to be addressed. First names may well be acceptable, but let them decide, or ask their caregiver, who knows them best.

Ask when is the best time to visit. Some people are "morning people" and others are better in the afternoon or evening; also each home, whether private or a nursing or care home, has its routines.

Check the practical details, such as whether the person needs a hearing aid or spectacles, and make sure they have them available and use them. I remember a lady in one of our homes who rarely remembered to wear her hearing aid, and carers would ask her, automatically, "Bridget, where is your hearing aid?" It was always in her cardigan pocket.

If you are engaging in devotions, or any spiritual activity, use the version of the Bible and the types of hymns that the person is familiar with. "How Great Thou Art" is more meaningful to older people than the more modern, "How Great is Our God", for example, and the old King James Version than more modern translations. This is very important, as older memories stay intact longer than later ones – remember, your preferences are irrelevant! It's what the person knows and relates to that matters.

The sense of touch can be important to some people with dementia. When she was a care home manager, Janet says she rarely sat next to someone for more than a few minutes without a hand reaching out to her. Again, check with the caregiver or the carer at the home. If the individual likes to hold hands, do so very gently, remembering the fragility of old age.

During your visit

Take notice of the person's background in the way you speak and pray. Some may prefer prayers read from the *Book of Common Prayer*, whereas some prefer spontaneous prayers. Reading familiar prayers can be a great comfort when someone is struggling with uncertainty.

Keep each session brief and direct. Sit close, if

appropriate, and maintain good eye contact and a relaxed, friendly expression. People with dementia are particularly sensitive to body language and unexpressed emotion.

Speak clearly, and not too quickly – but don't shout. Don't labour your speech at all. Be consistent in all you do and say, and avoid hurrying. Don't make quick changes of activity or topics. Take everything a step at a time – think linearly.

Never condescend or "talk across" them: never scold or correct. Remember, their cognitive abilities are damaged. Your visit is meant to encourage and uplift, not create turmoil and anxiety. Focus on their remaining abilities, and do things in small steps.

Do not feel obliged to challenge their version of reality. As the condition progresses, memories are gradually lost, beginning with the latest. It may be that the sufferer is living in a world that is in the past, but it is not an imagined world. They are not being delusional: their world is very real even though it belongs to the past. Look for meaning in what they say and do; try looking beneath the words. If the person says something irrational, perhaps even "gibberish", be respectful and try to read their body language. Always treat them with love and concern. If possible, use their "errors" as a stepping-stone for meaningful contact.

Remember, keep it simple, keep it short and keep it sweet! Don't overload with information. And don't be afraid to repeat things, but do so gently, and with patience. If the person remembers one simple truth that encourages them, that will be a great blessing.

In coming to a spiritual activity, such as praying, reading from the Bible or singing a hymn, tell them clearly what you are about to do. Repeat yourself gently if they wander off onto a different subject. Tell them when you are going to sing, and try to get them to join in. You will have found out in advance what hymns or songs are relevant to them. We all love our old favourites, and when you have dementia these old favourites are touchstones for happy memories and feelings. If you do use familiar hymns and verses and you see that some of the people are saying them with you, get them to repeat the words out loud with you.

Speak often about reassuring things. Loss of assurance and loss of confidence in God are not unusual in frailty and confusion. Encouragement from the Scriptures is wonderful, especially to answer guilt and fears. Make a note of Hebrews 13:5–6; 2 Timothy 2:19; Psalm 71:18; John 20:28–30; Psalm 103:13–14; Romans 8:28–30, 34–37.

Draw on things they will know – for example, events of their childhood, Sunday School songs, and well-known Bible stories. Use pictures, soft toys or things they can handle, or memorabilia that will remind them. Much of ministry to confused people is about bringing back into their minds what they already know.

Speak frequently about Christ and the cross. Remind them of the glories of heaven, using the Scriptures when you can. John 14:1–3; Revelation 21:3–5; 22:1–4; Jude 24… there are many more you probably know well.

Towards the end of your short visit, summarize in a few words the main message you have brought them. It may be repeating again what you've said together earlier. It's always good to pray, briefly, at the end of your visit. Prayer brings calm and a sense of peace as the Holy Spirit ministers.

Love for the caregiver

Harry didn't forget the promise he'd made to himself that he would keep an eye on Linda, even after Frank had gone into care. Harry and his wife called for short visits, and they'd telephone her regularly, just keeping in touch. They made sure she stayed involved in church life and activities, and they talked about normal things as well as her feelings of guilt and concern about Frank. They talked, too, about their daughter, and how she had not been able to come to terms with her father's illness. It was several months before Linda felt she was beginning to come back to anything resembling a normal life. Although she thought she'd sleep for a whole weekend once she had the chance, it was some time before her normal sleep pattern reasserted itself. Harry and his wife and their friends helped Linda and Matthew through a grieving and healing process. Sometimes, when Linda would try to thank them, Harry would remind them that "It's a family thing. It's what we do for one another."

POINTS TO PONDER

- Settling a loved one in a care home can feel like a bereavement. But hold on to the thought that it's better for their well-being, as well as yours. Without the stress of 24/7 caring, many caregivers say they enjoy a better, more enriched relationship with their loved one.

- In a care or nursing home, there will be a number of carers, coming in to work after a rest. They will have more energy to meet the person's needs.

- Carers are trained especially to care for people with

dementia.

- Other Christians' presence is reassuring; sometimes it's comfortable to just sit alongside someone, without making conversation.
- Minister to the spirit of the person, with spiritual words and familiar Scripture verses.
- Remind yourself that we are pilgrims here. Unless the Lord returns sooner, fifty years from now most of us will be with the Lord, including you and your loved one, in better circumstances than we can ever imagine.

Chapter 12

Letter from America

*Do nothing out of selfish ambition or vain
conceit, but in humility consider others better than
yourselves. Each of you should look not only
to your own interests, but also to the interests of
others.*

PHILIPPIANS 2:3–4

There are often parallels between what is happening in the UK and the USA. As well as having the same language, we have similar demographics, including an ageing population with a rising incidence of dementia. Many of our readers will be American, so included here is a brief snapshot of what is happening with dementia in the United States.

Currently, every seventy-two seconds someone is diagnosed as having dementia in the USA, and that number will increase to one every thirty-three seconds in just over forty years. In just twenty years there will be an increase of 63 per cent in the number of people with dementia in the United States, according to the latest World Alzheimer's Report,[73] and the number of people with dementia is expected to increase from the current 5.5 million to something like 16 million.

America's elderly are a growing population, but one that tends to be concentrated in specific geographical areas. Areas where a high percentage of the population are over the age of sixty-five include not only retirement hotspots like Florida and the Southwest, but also places like the Great Plains, with a high level of out-migration of younger residents.[74]

There are retirement villages, where older people have built easy-to-maintain homes. There is one such village called "Sun City" near one of my sons in Menifee, California. It has homes with front gardens lined with green gravel that doesn't have to be mown, instead of green grass, and roadsigns warning drivers to watch out for the golf-cart-type buggies that many older people use to get around there. It also has a large assisted living scheme, with a frontage on the main street, and the stores stock many items for older people. As older people moved into the area, service industries accompanied them, along with younger people with children, and a ripple-like effect has seen the area sprawl enormously in the last few years. But Sun City still has a predominantly elderly feel to it, and there are long lines of older people at the dispensing counters in the stores at certain times of day. The public health system in America is not like ours in the UK, and I often wonder how these older folk can afford to pay for the medication they are collecting. It has always seemed odd, to me, that a country with the wealth of America – that has sent aid liberally to so many other countries – does not have a medical care system that includes everybody. It increases my appreciation of our National Health Service, even with all its imperfections.

Carol Bradley Bursack is an American writer and columnist who, over the span of two decades, cared for a neighbour and six elderly family members. Because of this experience she created an organization called "Minding Our Elders" and wrote a book which she calls a portable support group: *Minding Our Elders: Caregivers Share Their Personal Stories*.

It's a reminder that elderly people, including those with dementia, and their caregivers aren't alone. It is an intimate and powerful resource for caregivers, filled with true stories about seniors and ageing parents. Her sites, www.mindingourelders.com and www.mindingoureldersblogs.com include helpful resources as well as links to direct support. Towards the end of this chapter is information on the different forms of care available in the USA.

Here, Carol tells the story of her struggle to care for her father, whose war injury caused brain damage which eventually led to dementia:

Big man in a small world

"Thank you for believing in me." Dad looked straight at me, his hazel eyes taking on the blue tint of his new shirt. He looked clear and alive for that brief moment, as he said those words, but then quickly faded. Dementia once again claimed his brain.

My father had suffered a closed head injury during World War II. He lay in a coma for weeks, then came around and had to be taught to walk and talk once more. He recovered enough to rejoin his young family after the war, earn a college degree, father a third child and have a distinguished career.

Toward the end of his working years, around the age of sixty, his brain began to give him problems. He took a demotion in his job until he could retire, and with less stress, he still enjoyed life well into his seventies. Then more fluid started building up behind the scar tissue left by the injury. Surgery was recommended to drain off that fluid. While that type of surgery was generally successful, it was a disaster for Dad. He came out of it totally demented.

We, his devastated family, had to place him in a nursing home. There was an excellent home just blocks from where I lived, and close to the apartment where he and my mother lived, so she could easily drive to see him. My uncle was already at that nursing home, so my mother and I would visit daily. Eventually my mother also needed nursing care and moved to the same home.

Dad's dementia was a journey for me, as I fought the accepted psychiatric practice of the time. First of all, the drug the psychiatrist prescribed made Dad horribly paranoid. It was an anti-psychotic medication, and on it his life was unbearable. I pleaded with his doctors, and eventually his medication was changed and he improved a little. It was obvious, however, that he would never get well. Dad had come out of surgery with a brain that didn't work as it had before, and which affected his sense of identity and seemed to have altered his personality.

There were occasional, glorious moments, however, when Dad would have a sudden moment of clarity, such as when he thanked me for validating his sense of reality and not challenging him. Alzheimer's patients, too, can have these moments of clarity. These precious moments seem to come from nowhere and can't be predicted.

Another time Dad's face cleared – it was always physically obvious when these rare moments occurred, as his whole demeanour momentarily normalized – and he said to me, "My universe has gotten so small."

Indeed it had. Let me explain. My Dad was a curious man whose interests took him into studying subjects as diverse as space travel and archaeology. Growing up in the twenties, he read novels telling of people landing on the moon. During my childhood, he told me that would one day really happen. It did.

He participated in an archaeological dig one summer out on the searing prairie lands of North Dakota, living with Native Americans and learning the mysteries of civilizations past.

Dad learned to speak Spanish, as he wanted to deliver health care to migrant workers who came to the prairie for fall harvest. He felt someone needed to speak their language, and at that time, few people in our area did. He brought, during his work, innovative thought that made him nationally known in the field that chose him when he was a young military man recovering from a brain injury – that of public health.

During his early years he had, for a short time, studied medicine. Mathematics not being his strong point, he changed directions (prodded by the war). He also took many other courses from different universities. He loved to learn. He eventually earned his degree in sociology.

After Dad's surgery, these memories were so real to him that they took on an importance that seemed unrealistic to people who didn't know him. He seemed to be living more in the past than in the present. But he wasn't fantasizing about his achievements or his past, because these were things that had really happened. And as time passed, I discovered that Dad was happiest when I entered his world, and agreed with his sense of things.

One doctor disagreed with me violently about "giving in" to Dad's "fantasies". I was to redirect him and bring him back into the real world. That was the only way to handle this. To "lie" to him and give in to his thoughts was wrong. This was psychiatric thought at the time, but when I tried doing as suggested, I didn't need a degree in anything to tell me that this method was doing nothing for Dad but putting him through unnecessary misery. What harm if he thought he was working in tandem with an Entomology professor at a North Dakota university? What harm would it do if I bought him a director's wand and let him direct the music on the television show? What harm, I asked the doctor, would my method do? He was never going to get well. Why not give him some satisfaction? To me, what I was doing was enlarging Dad's universe. He seemed to need a purpose and I was trying to help him fulfil that need.

Fast forward five years. A different psychiatrist was visiting with Dad as I came into his room. He asked me, "Where did you learn that?" I knew what he meant. Where had I learned to go with the flow? Where had I learned that it was senseless to argue with a person who could not reason? Indeed, instinct and inner guidance was all I had to go on. I was not going to torture my Dad with some technique that would only make him miserable.

As the years have passed, and elder care has become my career, Alzheimer's has been a large part of my work. And I have long believed that, once a person with Alzheimer's gets to a stage where logic no longer works, getting into their world saves much misery.

This can become a very tricky issue, however, when the person with dementia is caught in a terrifying frame of mind. Dad saw a news broadcast on television (against my direct orders), and it contained some war footage. Immediately, Dad decided there was a war in the streets of our town. No matter what I said, he thought I was lying. I asked him to go to the window with me and look. He refused. Of course, his memories of World War II were a part of this, but mainly it was the terror of knowing his present vulnerability and not knowing how to avoid "capture". Penny Garner's SPECAL method hadn't been developed then.

People with Alzheimer's and other dementias often get mistrustful. They forget where they put things, or have forgotten even the decade in which they are living, so they wonder why they can't find something they owned thirty years ago. If it's not there then someone took it. And that someone is probably you.

One woman at the nursing home where my parents lived constantly accused the nursing assistants of stealing her sweater. She had a favourite red sweater. Occasionally, it had to be wrestled away from her to get it washed. She was upset the whole time it was gone, even though she had several other sweaters. One of the aides, poorly paid as she was, took a whole day to track down a red sweater as similar as possible to the one the woman owned, so they could all have some peace. I think the woman had an inkling that there was something fishy about the substitute red sweater, but she couldn't pin it down, so the little trick worked. They could then wash the precious red sweater when it was warranted.

Thankfully, little things like what this aide did are now considered acceptable by forward-thinking specialists here in the US. Joining a dementia-afflicted elder in his or her world is now encouraged by many professionals. The empathetic care of people with dementia that has been introduced in the UK, in an earlier chapter referred to as SPECAL, reminds me of the work now being done in the US by the Pioneer Network. From their website at www.pioneernetwork.net, a reader can find out more about these remarkable folks. The website explains their mission, beginning with these words:

> Pioneer Network was formed in 1997 by a small group of prominent professionals in long-term care to advocate for person-directed care. This group called for a radical change in the culture of aging so that when our grandparents, parents – and ultimately ourselves –

go to a nursing home or other community-based setting
it is to thrive, not to decline.

This group readily recognizes that people with dementia
have a right to be treated with respect and dignity. And now,
fortunately, many if not most psychiatrists here recognize that
part of this treatment is to stop arguing with a person with
dementia about whose reality is right. When someone has
dementia, what their minds tell them is as real as what our
minds tell us. What right do we have to continually tell them
they are wrong?

What at one time was considered demeaning is now
rightly viewed as respectful. We, who are supposedly blessed
(for now) with brains that view the true reality of an issue (can
anyone really do this without bias?), have the responsibility to
mentally join the person with dementia, wherever they are.

For me, that meant that Dad's nursing home room was
his office. I was his office manager. I also delivered his "mail",
which often contained letters from dignitaries and celebrities,
as well as requests for his enormous talents in many fields. This
was something I could do for my wonderful father. I could
validate the reality of his world. All I could say to his "thank
you" to me was, "I'm happy for the privilege. It's the least I
can do."

Thank God that medical thought is slowly catching up
with the hearts of many of us who have had loved ones with
dementia and have known instinctively how to handle their
needs. And thank God for programs like SPECAL and the
people in the Pioneer Network and other programs who are
championing this supercharged person-centred care.

For our elders, and others with dementia, deserve no
less. They are people with a legacy of life behind them. Their

dignity must be honoured if we are to care for them well.

About the type of care available, Carol says:

Our government says they want people to stay in their homes longer and there are more programs in place to help pay for care, but there's still a long way to go here, too. Our main types of care are:

Nursing homes, with skilled nursing care

Many of these homes are adding adult day care. This is not skilled nursing and is just as it says, only for the day. Still, it's a great option, and if the day care is attached to a nursing home – some are and some aren't – a nurse is available from the home. If not, and for some this has less stigma and is preferable, there is no nursing care.

In-home care agencies can fill in gaps

Here too, it gets complicated. In-home care agencies nearly all provide "custodial care", though what they do varies with training. This care cost is seldom covered by government funding unless the person is on Medicaid (very low income). Then, sometimes some funds are available. In most cases, these custodial caregivers can't even give medication. They can witness the person taking it, but that is all. Some of these agencies have nursing care, too. Then, a nurse goes to the home for whatever care is needed in that way. If a person is discharged from the hospital, they often get some in-home nursing services paid for by Medicare.

Assisted living

This is a group environment, but does not generally include nursing. However, if someone lives in assisted living, an in-home agency can be independently hired for this assistance. Assisted living contracts vary and they aren't as well regulated as nursing homes. Some provide more services than others.

Residential care

These are homes that are licensed to care for a small number of people. Some like this, as it seems more "home like". They may care for a couple of people or up to a dozen or more, depending on licensing. They would not generally have a nurse on staff, but they could. Each is different. I would expect most don't, but they may hire an in-home care agency to help.

We have some parish nurse and "block nurse" (pretty much the same thing) programs available in some areas. This is very nice. They go to people's homes. Many also provide custodial care. These are very popular where they exist, but as with so much, it's spotty.

Bob Tell is the author of *Dementia Diary: A Caregiver's Journal*, and he runs an informative blog, *The Caregiver Chronicles* (http://caregiverchronicle.blogspot.com), based on material in the book. If you live in America you may find both his book and his blog helpful. In his 4 July 2009 posting, entitled 'Keyword Glossary for Alzheimer's/Dementia Services', he gave the following information about Medicaid and Medicare homes:

MEDICAID NURSING HOMES – Medicaid is the national program for financing health care to the poor. The cost of elderly care is so high that many patients run through their savings and are nearly destitute by the time nursing home care is needed. Elderly patients needing skilled nursing care who cannot afford a private nursing home may qualify for Medicaid. While not all nursing homes accept patients on Medicaid, many do. Guidance for families in this situation can be found on the internet by using this keyword phrase.

MEDICARE NURSING HOMES – Medicare is part of our Social Security system and provides financing for medical services to most citizens over the age of 65 regardless of their ability to pay. However, not all nursing homes accept payment from Medicare because that government program is quite limited with respect to long term care benefits. These homes fear that when Medicare benefits run out, they'll have to continue to provide care without receiving compensation for services rendered. Nevertheless, many nursing homes are open to admitting Medicare patients for at least the short term – and some will permit such patients to remain if they become Medicaid eligible. It's important to obtain this information up front as you go about researching nursing homes for your loved one.

HOSPICE CARE – Most folks are now familiar with this wonderful care concept for dying patients and their families. It was pioneered in England in the 1960s, promoted by Elizabeth Kubler-Ross's work on death and dying, and is now widely available throughout the United States. Medicare currently pays for most elderly patients requiring hospice care.

In summary, the main types of care are:

219

- *Nursing home:* skilled nursing 24/7 where people live.
- *Assisted living:* communal living that can be as swanky as a resort or much more humble. Expensive and paid for out of pocket in most cases. Few have a nurse on staff.
- *In-home care agencies:* some offer nursing, others don't.
- *Small assisted living homes that could be called residential:* these seldom have nursing, but would hire in-home nurses when needed. Some are licensed to give medication but can't "break the skin". It all depends on training and licensing.
- *Adult day care* (and a very few night cares as an alternative are popping up): they may have a nurse handy if they are attached to a nursing home. Otherwise, they likely have an in-home company on call, but the charge would be extra.
- *Medicaid nursing homes, Medicare nursing homes, and hospice care.*

POINTS TO PONDER

- Close family members who are caregivers often know much about the past experiences of the person with dementia. Make sure the relevant information is given to others, particularly carers, so they understand more of the inner world of the person.
- *Contented Dementia*, the book that describes SPECAL, should also be available in bookstores in the United States. If it isn't, you can obtain it from Amazon.com.
- If you haven't read *Could It Be Dementia? Losing Your Mind Doesn't Mean Losing Your Soul* (by Louise Morse and Roger Hitchings), we recommend you purchase it from Amazon, Barnes & Noble, or any Christian bookstore.

- When looking for help in America, it helps to type in the keywords into search engines such as Google, Ask or Yahoo. Some of these keywords will be: adult day care; residential care; home care; assisted living; nursing home; skilled nursing home; Medicaid nursing homes; Medicare nursing homes.

Chapter 13

Fellowship – the Best Preventative

*So in Christ we who are many form one body, and
each member belongs to all the others.*

ROMANS 12:5

If we could fast forward say, ten years, what could we expect to see? If today's trends continue we could see much of the stigma and dread surrounding dementia disappear. Not only will more be understood about the illness, but when we reach the stage where one in three families are impacted by dementia, it will lose its uniquely horrifying aura. If the government's dementia strategy rolls out as promised, there will be no more battling on alone and fighting for help by caregivers, and if the SPECAL way of care is taken up, as it looks like being, sufferers will be able to live and die with a measure of peace and contentment. Dementia is where cancer was fifty years ago, but many cancers are now treatable and a diagnosis is not necessarily a death sentence. My brother fought a type of cancer for years, but something hardly heard of as late as ten years ago – a stem-cell transplant – has completely transformed his life. And like dementia, the causes of most cancers are not clear at all. Research continues into treatment and prevention of dementia, and the main question we're often asked at seminars is, "What's the best way of preventing it?"

There are many practical things we can do to keep as fit as we can. Exercise has been shown to have beneficial effects on the brain. A study two years ago at the University of Kansas, USA, showed a clear and significant link between physical fitness and greater volume of the hippocampus, the area of your brain that stores memory, and is affected by dementia. Subjects with poor fitness levels showed more pronounced signs of atrophy – shrinking of this part of the brain. Simply walking is good. One study implied that walking produced a "wave effect" that was positive for the brain.

When it comes to an all-round plan, I haven't come across a better one than that put forward by Dr Majid Fotuhi, Neurology Consultant at the Alzheimer's Disease Research Center at John Hopkins Hospital in Baltimore. I mentioned it in *Could It Be Dementia?* and it's so good that it's worth repeating. It was summarized by Herb Denenberg, a former Pennsylvania insurance commissioner and professor at the Wharton School, and a long-time Philadelphia journalist and consumer advocate.[75]

- *One:* Take control of your blood pressure. Long-term high blood pressure reduces the blood flow to the brain and other organs. Reduction in blood flow means a reduction in nutrient supply, and the end result is that the brain is more susceptible to Alzheimer's. In addition, several studies show that high blood pressure in mid-life means poor brain function later in life.
- *Two:* Make sure you have good levels of cholesterol. High levels of cholesterol not only lead to heart disease but also to memory and thinking problems, and even Alzheimer's. So do what you have to do to lower cholesterol, including

lifestyle changes involving exercise and diet, and if all else fails, drug treatment.

- *Three:* Check your B12 and homocysteine levels. Low levels of certain vitamins, including B-12 and folate, lead to high homocysteine levels, which in turn is associated with Alzheimer's.

- *Four:* Eat a diet rich in fruit and vegetables and add some wine. You probably already know that a diet rich in fruits, vegetables, whole grains and dairy products reduces heart disease. The typical American diet – and probably the typical British diet too – is said to be high in fats and is linked to high blood pressure and mini-strokes, which contribute to deterioration of memory. There is also evidence that drinking a moderate amount of wine a day reduces the risk of developing dementia. The reason for the beneficial effects is not fully understood.

- *Five:* Protect your brain from injury. Head trauma has been linked to Alzheimer's, so do what you can to minimize your chances of trauma. That means using seatbelts, wearing helmets when biking, skateboarding, horseback riding etc., and taking other steps to protect the brain and minimize serious injuries.

- *Six:* Check your eyes and ears – sharpen your senses. To receive, process and remember you have to have eyes and ears that are working. This relationship is so obvious that it is often ignored, along with that other great body of recommendation called common sense. Poor vision and hearing adversely affect memory and brain function.

- *Seven:* Exercise. Low levels of physical activity lead to memory loss and just about every other kind of health problem there is. Exercise is one of the master keys to health and to preserving and protecting memory and brainpower. Exercise, or simply keeping moving, has been called the most important step anyone should take to stay healthy. (Even a moderate amount of physical exercise can increase brain volume in older adults, according to a study at the University of Illinois at Urbana Champaign.)[76]

- *Eight:* Your brain – use it or lose it! Just as disuse of muscles leads to their atrophy, so does disuse of memory and brainpower.

- *Nine:* Socialize – become a more interesting person. Studies show that men with "high productivity and an active social lifestyle were seven times less likely to develop dementia" (Denenberg did not footnote this study).

- *Ten:* Beware of depression and stress. Stress and depression cause memory loss. You have to learn to handle stress and treat depression. You have to see the glass half full, not half empty, and appreciate what you have rather than mourn over what you don't have.

- *Eleven:* Denenberg would add one more step – *sleep*. Some sleep experts are now saying that getting enough sleep will one day be recognized as being just as important as exercise and a healthy diet.

According to some, we should be adding vitamin and food supplements to our diet, particularly fish oils and Vitamin D. There's an epidemic of low levels of Vitamin D at the moment, though nobody seems to know why that should be. Vitamin D is made by our bodies as they are exposed to sunshine, but even in the sunny city of Greenville, South Carolina, Dr Jana Morse reports alarmingly low levels. It's important because Vitamin D is one of the "kick starter" elements for a number of vital functions, and there have been reports that a deficiency could be linked to dementia. Here in the UK we are not tested for levels of vital nutrients, as a rule, until we are ill, but there are private practitioners who can do tests. Again, it's good to begin with your family doctor.

Secrets of a healthy, long life

Researchers examine people who have lived longer than usual to see if they can discover the secret of their good health. They want to know, is it genetics, or a healthy lifestyle, or some combination of the two? An example was a Spanish man who died aged 114. A research team at the Universitat Autonoma de Barcelona examined him at the age of 113, looking particularly at his bones and his lifestyle. He enjoyed a Mediterranean diet, a temperate climate, had cycled daily until the age of 103, and only gave up looking after the family orchard when he reached 102. Researchers also looked at other members of his family: a 101-year-old brother, two daughters aged eighty-one and seventy-seven, and a nephew aged eighty-five, all of them born and still living in a small town on the island of Menorca. They found his bones were in excellent condition, and neither the man nor his family had any genes that could be implicated in their long lives. None of them had dementia.

The researchers did not rule out the possibility that genetic mutations could positively influence longevity, but they did point out that the excellent health of this family was probably due to their lifestyle, which included their diet, a lack of stress and regular physical activity.

Scientists say the secret lies not so much in the genes, but in the genetic expression – in other words, the way they play out. Tom Kitwood, the light-bearer in dementia, said that our genetic inheritance was simply a background on which other causes operate: "A paper pattern does not cause the making of a dress. At the very least we need that view of causation that looks for the set of interacting conditions – all necessary but none sufficient in themselves – that are required for an event to occur."[77]

Similar observations to the Spanish study were made in a study of a group of Italians who emigrated to America in the late 1800s. Eventually around 2,000 of them settled in a village they'd built on the lines of the one they'd left in Italy, calling it Roseta. The nearest neighbouring villages had different languages – English, Welsh and German – which tended to exclude the villagers of Roseta, Pennsylvania, who retained their close-knit way of living along with their local Italian dialect. They may never have been heard of except for the discovery that they led extraordinarily long lives. They did not develop heart disease, or other ailments of old age, and this attracted researchers, led by Dr Stewart Wolf, who thought that at first, it must be due to a genetic inheritance. Wolf and a sociologist named John Bruhn, with the help of medical students and sociology graduate students, interviewed every person in Roseta aged twenty-one and over, going from house to house. They found no suicide, no alcoholism, no drug addiction, and very little crime. There was no one on welfare. There were no peptic ulcers. "These people were dying of old age. That's it," said John Bruhn.[78]

The researchers looked at the Rosetans' diet, and found they were cooking with lard instead of with the much healthier olive oil they had used back in Italy. They had other unhealthy eating habits, and 41 per cent of their daily calories came from fat. Many of them smoked heavily, were overweight, and took very little exercise. Perplexed, researchers did other research, including examining other Rosetans, still living in Italy.

Eventually the only conclusion they could draw was that the Rosetans' longevity was not due to diet, or exercise, or genes, or location, but to the way they looked after one another:

> In transplanting the... culture of southern Italy to the hills of Eastern Pennsylvania, the Rosetans had created a powerful, protective social structure capable of insulating them from the pressures of the modern world. The Rosetans were healthy because of where they were *from*, because of the world they had created for themselves in their tiny little town in the hills.[79]

Among the reams of studies and advice about preventing dementia, one of the strongest themes to emerge confirms the Rosetan factor. Researchers at Rush University's Alzheimer's Disease Centre in Chicago found a link between feelings of loneliness and developing dementia, including Alzheimer's, in elderly people.[80] The risk of developing Alzheimer's rose by about 51 per cent for each extra point scored on the loneliness scale. A person with a loneliness rating of 3.2 had twice the Alzheimer's risk of someone with a low score of 1.4. A new study, published in the *Archives of Internal Medicine*, followed 906 older adults for about five years, and found that those with less social activity had a more rapid rate of motor function decline. And a one-point decrease in social activity was equivalent to being about five years older at the start of the study. Researchers said that translated to a 40 per cent higher risk of death and a 65 per cent higher risk of disability.[81]

In an intriguing first sentence, a press release from Health Day News said: "Sociable people who don't sweat the small stuff may be more likely to remember the small stuff as they age, suggests new research exploring the link between personality and the incidence of Alzheimer's Disease." The article quoted a study published in the journal *Neurology*, showing the growing body of evidence suggesting a link between personality traits, lifestyle and Alzheimer's disease. It found that people with active social lives were 50 per cent less likely to develop dementia.[82]

With our church fellowships, and our relationship with other believers, shouldn't we be enjoying active social lives – lives engaging with the family of God? We should be like "Jerusalem, a city built close together", as the psalmist said (Psalm 122:3). It sounds very much like Roseta in Pennsylvania. Many churches do have a close fellowship, but the pressures of modern-day life prevent many others doing the same. So it might be worth making healthy lifestyle choices as the dementia tsunami rolls in.

POINTS TO PONDER

- There have been three significant changes in dementia – reducing stigma, a government strategy and SPECAL, a new way of caring based on better understanding.
- A Mediterranean diet is considered the healthiest and is recommended for preventing dementia.
- Regular exercise, even simple walking, can help, too.
- Stay socially engaged – enjoy the family of God.

Organizations Offering Advice and Help

In the United Kingdom

Age Concern

Age Concern is the largest UK charity working with and for older people. The website provides information about local branches throughout Britain. A national helpline will give links to local branches.
Tel: 0800 009966
www.ageconcern.org.uk

Age Concern Cymru (Wales)

Ty John Pathy
13/14 Neptune Court
Vanguard Way
Cardiff
CF24 5PJ
Tel: 029 2043 1555
Email: enquiries@accymru.org.uk
www.accymru.org.uk

Age Concern Northern Ireland

3 Lower Crescent
Belfast
BT7 1NR
Tel: 028 9024 5729
Email: info@ageconcernni.org
www.ageconcernni.org

The Alzheimer's Society

The UK's leading care and research charity for people with dementia, their families and carers.
Devon House
58 St Katharine's Way
London
E1W 1JX
Tel: 020 7423 3500
Fax: 020 7423 3501
Email: enquiries@alzheimers.org.uk
www.alzheimers.org.uk

Carer's Allowance Unit

Department of Work and Pensions
Palatine House
Lancaster Road
Preston
Lancashire
PR1 1HB
Tel: 01253 856 123
www.direct.gov.uk/

Carers Christian Fellowship

The Carers Christian Fellowship aims to offer a link and support for Christians who are caring in some way for a relative, friend or neighbour. The Fellowship offers mutual support to fellow Christians by prayer and sharing the reality of the Christian experience in the middle of the stress of caring.

14 Cavie Close
Nine Elms
Swindon
Wiltshire
SN5 5XD
Tel: 01793 887068
www.carerschristianfellowship.org.uk

Care Quality Commission

The independent regulator of health and social care in England. All health and adult social care providers, who provide regulated activities, are required by law to register with the Care Quality Commission. The website shows ratings for homes in the UK.

Care Quality Commission National Correspondence
Citygate
Gallowgate
Newcastle upon Tyne
NE1 4PA
Tel: 03000 616161
Email: enquiries@cqc.org.uk
www.cqc.org.uk/

Carers UK

Carers UK is the voice of carers. The organization fights to obtain better support for carers.
20–25 Glasshouse Yard
London
EC1A 4JT
Tel: 020 7378 4999
Carers' Line: 0808 808 7777
Email: info@carersuk.org
www.carersuk.org/Contactus (for contacts in Ireland, Scotland and Wales)

Counsel and Care for Older People and their Carers

A national charity providing personalized, in-depth advice and information, aiming to ensure that everyone who asks for advice and information receives the support that they are entitled to.
Counsel and Care
Twyman House
16 Bonny Street
London
NW1 9PG
Tel: 020 7241 8555
Email: contact form on website
www.counselandcare.org.uk

Crossroads

Crossroads is a national network of local charities employing over 5,000 trained professionals. It provides flexible services to people of all ages and with a range of disabilities and health conditions. The website gives regional contact addresses

throughout the UK.
Caring for Carers
Crossroads Association
10 Regent Place
Rugby
Warwickshire
CV21 2PN
Tel: 0845 450 0350
www.crossroads.org.uk

Dementia Care Trust

This group aims to relieve mentally infirm elderly people by the provision of suitable accommodation, health care, counselling and other forms of assistance, and support for such persons in order to provide facilities to foster, encourage or experience a sense of independence in their mode of life or present living conditions.
Kingsley House
Greenbank Road
Bristol
BS5 6HE
Tel: 0117 952 5325
Fax: 0117 951 8213
www.brunelcare.org.uk

Dementia Care Partnership

Dementia Care Partnership (DCP) is a registered Newcastle-based charity which provides local services for people with dementia of all ages, including people from the black and minority ethnic communities. Currently DCP provides services in Northumberland, Gateshead and North Tyneside.
Bradbury Centre

Darrell Street,
Brunswick Village
Newcastle upon Tyne
NE13 7DS
Tel: 0191 217 1323
Fax: 0191 236 5778
Email: bradburycentre@dementiacare.org.uk
www.dementiacare.org.uk

DISC

The Dementia Information Service for Carers (based in Warwickshire). Advice and information for carers of older people with dementia.
Guideposts Trust
6 Tom Brown Street
Rugby
CV21 3JT
Tel: 0845 4379901
Email: info@disc.org.uk
www.disc.org.uk

for dementia

A national charity committed to improving the life of all people affected by dementia. for dementia also helps with Admiralty Nurses.
6 Camden High Street
London
NW1 0JH
Tel: 020 7874 7210
www.fordementia.org.uk

Dementia Voice

An organization responsible for the management and development of specialist care provision, research and training in the South-west.

Hillside Court
Batten Road
Bristol
BS5 8NL
Tel: 0870 192 4747
Fax: 0870 192 4748
Email: kim.warren@housing21.co.uk
www.dementia-voice.org.uk

Office of the Public Guardian

Supports and promotes decision-making for those who lack capacity or would like to plan for their future, within the framework of the Mental Capacity Act 2005.

Office of the Public Guardian
PO Box 15118
Birmingham
B16 6GX
Tel: 0300 456 0300
Email: customerservices@publicguardian.gsi.gov.uk
www.publicguardian.gov.uk/

Help the Aged

Advice and support. Their website provides information about local branches throughout Britain.
Tel: 020 7278 1114
Email: info@helptheaged.org.uk
www.helptheaged.org.uk

Holiday Care Service

A national charity dedicated to making tourism welcoming to all.
Tourism for All
c/o Vitalise
Shap Road Industrial Estate
Shap Road
Kendal
Cumbria
LA9 6NZ
Tel: 0845 124 9971
Email: info@tourismforall.org.uk
www.tourismforall.org.uk

PARCHE

Pastoral Action in Residential Care Homes for the Elderly. Meeting the spiritual needs of elderly people in care. PARCHE, together with Eastbourne churches, offers regional help and national training and envisioning for church teams.
St Elizabeth's Church
268 Victoria Drive
Eastbourne
BN20 8QX
Tel: 01323 438527
Email: PARCHEenquiries@hotmail.co.uk
www.parche.org.uk

Parish Nursing Ministries UK

Whole-person health care through the local church.
Red Helen Wordsworth
3 Barnwell Close
Dunchurch

Nr Rugby
Warwickshire
CV22 6QH
Tel: 01788 817292
www.parishnursing.co.uk

PDSG

Pick's Disease Support Group – Lewy Body Dementia. The PDSG charity is under the umbrella of the National Hospital for Neurology and Neurosurgery Development Foundation. Caring for people with frontotemporal dementia is hard; there are few facilities tailored for the younger sufferer and those are not always appropriate for people with frontotemporal dementia. The website provides regional links.
www.pdsg.org.uk

SPECAL

This dementia and Alzheimer's charity provides courses, services and advice.
The SPECAL Centre
Sheep Street
Burford
OX18 4LS
Email: help@specal.co.uk
www.specal.co.uk

The Princess Royal Trust for Carers

Provides support services in the UK, through its unique network of 144 independently managed Carers' Centres, eighty-five young carers' services and interactive websites.
142 Minories
London

EC3N 1LB
Tel: 0844 800 4361
Email: info@carers.org
www.carers.org

Registered Nursing Home Association

Formed in 1968, the RNHA campaigns strongly for high standards in nursing home care.
John Hewitt House
Tunnel Lane, off Lifford Lane
Kings Norton
Birmingham
B30 3JN
Tel: 0121 451 1088
Email: via website
www.rnha.co.uk/

Relatives and Residents Association

24 The Ivories
6–18 Northampton Street
London
N1 2HY
Tel (advice line): 020 7359 8136
Tel (admin.): 020 7359 8148
www.relres.org

Wandering in Dementia

A UK-wide service for carers and professionals looking after people with memory loss who are at risk of getting lost.
NHS Innovations South East
Harwell Innovation Centre
Building 173

Curie Avenue
Harwell International Business Centre
Didcot
Oxfordshire
OX11 0QG
Tel: 0845 8900200
Email: information@wanderingindementia.co.uk
www.wanderingindementia.com

In the USA

Alzheimer's Association

225 N. Michigan Avenue, Fl. 17
Chicago, IL 60601-7633
24/7 helpline: contact us for information, referral and support.
Tel: 1-800-272-3900
Tdd: 1-866-403-3073
Email: info@alz.org
www.alz.org/

American Association for Geriatric Psychiatry

7910 Woodmont Avenue, Suite 1050
Bethesda, MD 20814-3004
Tel: (301) 654-7850
www.aagpgpa.org

Minding our Elders

It is the mission of Minding Our Elders to shine a light on the isolation often felt by caregivers and seniors and to give them a voice. Informative website with links to others.

www.eldercarelink.com

www.mindingourelders.com/

Family Caregiver Alliance

National Center on Caregiving

180 Montgomery Street, Ste 1100

San Francisco, CA 94104

Tel: (800) 445-8106

(415) 434-3388

www.caregiver.org

National Alliance for Caregiving

4720 Montgomery Lane, 5th Floor

Bethesda, MD 20814

www.caregiving.org

National Institutes of Health and National Institute on Aging

An official US website with information and links.

Alzheimer's Disease Education and Referral Center (ADEAR)

PO Box 8250

Silver Spring, MD 20907-8250

Tel: (800) 438-4380

(301) 495-3311

www.nia.nih.gov/alzheimers

National Institute of Neurological Disorders and Stroke

National Institutes of Health

NIH Neurological Institute

PO Box 5801

Bethesda, MD 20824
Voice: (800) 352-9424 or (301) 496-5751
TTY (for people using adaptive equipment): (301) 468-5981
www.ninds.nih.gov

National Mental Health Association

Gives information and links to affiliate websites.
2000 North Beauregard Street, 6th Floor
Alexandria, VA 22311
Tel: (703) 684-7722
www.nmha.org/

Gerontological Society of America

Gives a list of other organizations.
www.geron.org/online.html

Mid-America Congress on Aging

Some different but interesting links, such as census data and
financial assistance organizations.
lgrossman.com/macareso.htm

www.thirteen.org/bid/resources.html

A website of the New York Public Broadcasting Service with
information and links focused on end-of-life care and issues.

In Australia

Alzheimer's Australia

The principal body providing support and advocacy for the
245,400 Australians living with dementia.

Alzheimer's Australia
PO Box 4019
Hawker ACT 2614
Tel: + (61) 2 6254 4233
National Dementia Helpline: 1800 100 500
www.alzheimers.org.au

Hammond Care

An independent Christian charity specializing in aged and dementia care.
Hammond Care
Level 2, 447 Kent Street
Sydney NSW 2000
Tel: 1300 426 666
Email: info@hammond.com.au
www.hammond.com.au

In New Zealand

Alzheimer's New Zealand

Provides support, information and contacts for people with dementia, their carers and family.
Alzheimer's New Zealand
Level 3, Adelphi Finance House
13 Courtenay Place
PO Box 3643
Wellington 6140
Tel: 04 381 2362
Email: nationaloffice@ alzheimers.org.nz
www.alzheimers.org.nz

International

www.alz.co.uk/alzheimers/languages.html

Page on UK Alzheimer's site with links for information in many other languages and countries.

www.healthandage.com/

This website has general information and also a page with contact information for Alzheimer's organizations in various countries.

DASNI

A worldwide organization by and for those suffering with dementia. Dementia Advocacy and Support Network International, since its founding in 2000, has evolved as an international group of people with dementia. Approximately one third of the members have dementia themselves.
www.dasninternational.org/

International Federation on Ageing

IFA serves as an advocate for the well-being of older persons around the world.
Dr Jane Barratt, Secretary General
IFA
Castleview Wichwood Towers (CWT)
351 Christie Street
Toronto, Ontario, M6G 3C3
Canada
Tel: 1-416-342-1655
Fax: 1-416-392-4157

Email: jbarratt@ifa-fiv.org
www.ifa-fiv.org/

The International Parish Nurse Resource Centre

Revd Dr Deborah L. Patterson
Executive Director
Deaconess Parish Nurse Ministries, LLC and
International Parish Nurse Resource Center
475 East Lockwood Avenue
Saint Louis, MO 63119
Tel: 314-918-2527
Email: dpatterson@eden.edu
www.parishnurses.org

Bibliography

Alzheimer's: Caring for Your Loved One, Caring for Yourself, Sharon Fish Mooney, Lion Hudson, 2008, ISBN 978 0 7459 5289 5

And Still the Music Plays: Stories of People with Dementia, Graham Stokes, Hawker Publications, 2008, ISBN 978 1 8747 9088 4

Contented Dementia: 24-hour Wraparound Care for Lifelong Well-being, Oliver James, Random House, 2008, ISBN 978 0 09190180 6

Could it be Dementia? Losing Your Mind Doesn't Mean Losing Your Soul, Louise Morse & Roger Hitchings, Monarch, 2008, ISBN 978 1 85424 825 1

Dementia Reconsidered: The Person Comes First, Tom Kitwood, Open University Press, 2008, ISBN 978 0 335 19855 9

Living Alone with Dementia – Alzheimer's: How to Keep Your Loved One in their Home As Long As Possible, Terry F. Townsend, Publish America, ISBN 978 1 60672 256 5

In a Strange Land: People with Dementia and the Local Church, Malcolm Goldsmith, 4M Publications, 2004, ISBN 978 0 95304946 2

Outliers: The Story of Success, Malcolm Gladwell, Penguin Books, 2009, ISBN 978 1 141 03625 0

Patients in Danger: The Dark Side of Medical Ethics, Gillian Craig, Medical Ethics Books, 2006, ISBN 978 0 95528400 7

Notes

1. www.alzheimers.org.uk
2. Louise Morse & Roger Hitchings, *Could it be Dementia? Losing Your Mind Doesn't Mean Losing Your Soul*, Monarch, 2008.
3. Christine Bryden, *Who Will I Be when I Die?*, Jessica Kingsley Publishers, 2005.
4. *The Guardian*, 12 October 2008.
5. *The Daily Telegraph*, 7 October 2008.
6. *Daily Mail*, 1 October 2009.
7. Nuffield Council on Bioethics, *Dementia: Ethical Issues*, October 2009.
8. *Daily Mail*, 1 October 2009.
9. Tom Kitwood, *Dementia Reconsidered*, Open University Press, 2008, p. 19.
10. http://www.guardian.co.uk/lifeandstyle/2008/aug/02/oliver.james.dementia
11. Oliver James, *Contented Dementia*, Vermilion, 2008, p. 119.
12. www.specal.co.uk (website); help@specal.co.uk (email support team). Address: The SPECAL Centre, Sheep Street, Burford, OX18 4LS.
13. Graham Stokes, *And Still the Music Plays*, Hawker Publications, 2008, p. 79.
14. Deuteronomy 33:27
15. Stokes, *And Still the Music Plays*, p. 111.

16. Stokes, *And Still the Music Plays*, p. 119.
17. Stokes, *And Still the Music Plays*, p. 128.
18. Carl Rogers, *Client-Centred Therapy*, Constable, 2000.
19. Interview in the *Guardian*, August 2008.
20. Dementia and SPECAL, 7 August 2008, BBC Radio 4.
21. http://www.mysteinbach.ca/blogs/?s=Dementia+-+Living+NOW
22. http://archpsyc.ama-assn.org/cgi/content/abstract/64/7/802
23. The *Independent*, 10 June 2009.
24. Professor of Mental Health and Ageing at King's College, London, and a Department of Health adviser.
25. G. W. Taylor's 'scientific management theory'.
26. http://www.communitycare.co.uk/
27. *Daily Mail*, 3 July 2009.
28. Malcolm Goldsmith, *In a Strange Land... People with Dementia and the Local Church*, 4M Publications, 2004.
29. 'Vacant Mind, Busy Brain', *New Scientist*, 8 November 2008.
30. *The Journal of Gerontology Series B: Psychological Sciences and Social Sciences*, September 2009.
31. Tom Kitwood, *Dementia Reconsidered*, Open University Press, 2008, p. 19.
32. *The Brain that Changes Itself*, Penguin, 2007.
33. Kitwood, *Dementia Reconsidered*, p. 63.
34. *Remembering Home: Rediscovering the Self in Dementia*, Johns Hopkins University Press, 2008.
35. Oliver James, *Contented Dementia*, Vermilion, 2008, p. 41.
36. Morse & Hitchings, *Could it Be Dementia?*
37. www.alz.co.uk/havedementia/lifedementia.html
38. UCLA's Semel Institute of Neuroscience and Human Behaviour, study in the journal *Stroke*, 2008, and

University of Melbourne in Australia, published in *Journal of the American Medical Association*, 2008.

39. http://www.reuters.com/article/healthnews/idUSTRE53T5ZH20090430

40. Sharon Fish Mooney, Lion Hudson, 2008.

41. Martin Graham, *Sizzling Faith*, Kingsway, 2006.

42. http://www.dare2share.org/devotions/do-you-believe-that/

43. *New York Times*, 14 June 2009.

44. James, *Contented Dementia*, p. 5.

45. Stokes, *And Still the Music Plays*, p. 155.

46. Stokes, *And Still the Music Plays*, p. 92.

47. *Non-Pharmacological Therapies for the Treatment of Behavioural Symptoms*, Alzheimer's Society.

48. 'Finger on the Pulse', *Daily Telegraph*, 22 June 2009.

49. Terry Pratchett at the Alzheimer's Research Trust, 2009.

50. *Paisley Daily Express*, 17 August 2009.

51. James, *Contented Dementia*, p. 152.

52. Kitwood, *Dementia Reconsidered*, p. 36.

53. Stokes, *And Still the Music Plays*, p. 174.

54. http://www.caring.com/articles/alzheimers-spiritual-activities

55. *Daily Telegraph*, 8 November 2008.

56. http://www.thefreedictionary.com/maze

57. *The Mail on Sunday*, 25 October, 2009.

58. Nuffield Council on Bioethics, *Dementia: Ethical Issues*, October 2009, Executive Summary.

59. Laing & Buisson, *Care of the Elderly*, July 2008.

60. http://www.internurse.com

61. http://www.statistics.gov.uk/

62. http://www.telegraph.co.uk/health/healthnews/6127514/Sentenced-to-death-on-the-NHS.html

63. Gillian Craig (ed.), *Patients in Danger: the Dark Side of Medical Ethics (Challenging Medical Ethics, Vol. 2)*, Enterprise House, 2006, p. v.

64. *Daily Telegraph*, 3 September 2009.

65. *Daily Telegraph*, 18 September 2008.

66. *Daily Mail*, 14 October 2009.

67. *Daily Mail*, 14 October 2009.

68. *Daily Telegraph*, 26 March 2009.

69. *Daily Mail*, 24 October 2009.

70. Goldsmith, *In a Strange Land*, p. 160.

71. *Quad City Times*, Iowa, 4 April 2009.

72. Deirdre Reilly, www.thepatriotledger.com, 26 March 2009.

73. Published by Alzheimer's Disease International (ADI), 2009.

74. www.censusscope.org

75. Denenberg, 'Ten Steps to Protect Your Memory and Brain', Special in the *Evening Bulletin*, 29 September 2006.

76. http://www.news.uiuc.edu/news/06/1120exercise.html

77. Kitwood, *Dementia Reconsidered*, p. 32.

78. Malcolm Gladwell, *Outliers: the story of success*, Penguin Books, 2009, p. 7.

79. Gladwell, *Outliers*, p. 9.

80. Archives of General Psychiatry, February 2007, www.rush.edu/webapps/MEDREL/servlet/NewsRelease?ID=844 - 32k -

81. www.webmd.com/healthy-aging/news20090622/solitude-speeds-effects-of-ageing

82. *Neurology*, 20 January 2009.

Topic Index

Contact Pilgrim Homes:

Pilgrim Homes
175 Tower Bridge Road
London
SE1 2AL
Tel: 0300 303 1400

www.pilgrimhomes.org.uk
info@pilgrimhomes.org.uk